ADDISON-WESLEY

QUEST 2000

EXPLORING MATHEMATICS

Randall I. Charles   David C. Brummett   Ricki Wortzman
Lalie Harcourt   Carne S. Barnett   Brendan Kelly

▲▼▲ Addison-Wesley Publishing Company

Menlo Park, California • Reading, Massachusetts • New York
Don Mills, Ontario • Wokingham, England • Amsterdam • Bonn
Paris • Milan • Madrid • Sydney • Singapore • Tokyo
Seoul • Taipei • Mexico City • San Juan

The Professional Team

Contributing Authors

Elisabeth Javor, Los Angeles, California
Alma Ramirez, Oakland, California
Freddie Lee Renfro, Bay Town, Texas
Mary M. Soniat-Thompson, New Orleans, Louisiana

Multicultural Advisors

Barbara Fong, Atherton, California
Jeanette Haseyama, San Diego, California
James Hopkins, Seattle, Washington
Lyn Tejada Mora, San Diego, California
Glenna Yee, Oakland, California
Teresa Walter, Encinitas, California
Roger E. W-B Olsen, San Francisco, California

Technology Advisors

Cynthia Dunham, Framingham, Massachusetts
Diana Nunnaley, Maynard, Massachusetts
Fred Crouse, Centreville, Nova Scotia
Flick Douglas, North York, Ontario
Susan Siedman, Toronto, Ontario
Evelyn Woldman, Framingham, Massachusetts

Editorial Coordination: McClanahan & Company

Design: McClanahan & Company

Cover Design: The Pushpin Group

ISBN: 0-201-84005-7

4 5 6 7 8 9 10 - VH - 99 98 97 96

Table of Contents

Unit 1: Discovering Patterns and Relationship

Launch	How can we use patterns to predict?	vi-1
Activity 1	Patterns Are Everywhere!	2-4
Activity 2	How Many Does It Take?	5-6
Activity 3	Growing Designs	7-10
Activity 4	Do the Hand Squeeze!	11-12
Activity 5	Number Crunchers	13-15
	People, Society, and Mathematics: Going Around in Circles, Squares, and Triangles	16-17
Activity 6	The Number Rule Game	18-19
Activity 7	What's the Best Deal?	20-21
Activity 8	Popcorn Graphs	22-23
Culminating Work	Experimenting with a Pendulum	24-25

Unit 2: Exploring Tessellations

Launch	What shapes cover completely?	26-27
Activity 1	Any Designs On It?	28
Activity 2	Cover Ups!	29-30
	People, Society, and Mathematics: The Latest in Home Fashions	31
Activity 3	Plane Covers	32-33
Activity 4	Tessellation Combinations	34-35
Culminating Work	A Puzzling Problem	36-37

Unit 3: Reasoning with Operations

Launch	How can we use operations?	38-39
Activity 1	Pizza Party	40-41
Activity 2	Peas Share!	42
Activity 3	Range Rover	43
	Target Game	44-45
Activity 4	The Great Divide	46-47
Activity 5	Yodos, Modos, and Hodos	48-49
Activity 6	Front Seats and Back Seats	50
	People, Society, and Mathematics: Eight-Year-Old Carl	51
Activity 7	Jiminy Cricket!	52-53
Activity 8	Name that Number!	54
Activity 9	What Numbers Are We?	55
Culminating Work	Fun Fund Raising	56-57

Unit 4: Exploring Fractional Parts

Launch	How can we show and use fractions?	58–59
Activity 1	From Finish to Start	60–61
Activity 2	How Now, Brown Cow?	62–63
Activity 3	Let's Go on a Fraction Hunt	64–65
Activity 4	A Typical Day in the Life of Otto Upside Down	66–67
Activity 5	Lots of Links	68–69
	People, Society, and Mathematics: Fractions of Time	70
Activity 6	Model Trains, Model Fractions	71
Culminating Work	Keep on Sliding	72–73

Unit 5: Building Rational Number Sense

Launch	How can we show and use decimals?	74–75
Activity 1	Tenths Around Us	76–77
Activity 2	The Decimal Place Value Game	78–79
Activity 3	Eating Out	80–81
Activity 4	More Money	82–83
	People, Society, and Mathematics: It's a 10!	84
Activity 5	Estimate and Solve	85–87
Activity 6	The Missing Factor Game	88–89
Culminating Work	The Effect of a Surface on Ball Bounce Height	90–91

Unit 6: Collecting and Analyzing Data

Launch	What patterns can we see in data?	92–93
Activity 1	Little Drops of Water	94–96
Activity 2	Beat the Clock	97–99
Activity 3	Some Like it Hot, Some Like it Cold	100–102
Activity 4	Long Ago Lengths	103–105
Activity 5	Deer Friends	106–108
	People, Society, and Mathematics: Information from Cords to Cards	109
Activity 6	Oh, Say Can You See	110–111
Culminating Work	The Time in a Week	112–113

Unit 7: Making Predictions

Launch	What is a good sample?	114–115
Activity 1	Four Out of Five Students Love This Page	116–117
Activity 2	Predicting How Many	118
	People, Society, and Mathematics: Making Predictions	119
Activity 3	The Sample Game	120–121
Activity 4	Common Letters	122–123
Activity 5	How Do We Compare?	124–125
Culminating Work	Taking a School Opinion Survey	126–127

Unit 8: Describing Percents

Launch	What is percent?	128–129
Activity 1	Percents All Around	130–131
Activity 2	Designing Floor Plans	132–133
Activity 3	Estimating Floor Space	134–135
Activity 4	Percents Line Up	136–137
	People, Society, and Mathematics:	
	Healthy By Percent	138–139
Activity 5	The Chance of Rain or Snow	140–142
Activity 6	The Closest Percent	143
Culminating Work	Analyzing a Newspaper	144–145

Unit 9: Exploring Positive and Negative Numbers

Launch	How can we use negative numbers?	146–147
Activity 1	It's a Matter of Degree	148
	People, Society, and Mathematics:	
	Absolutely the Coldest!	149
Culminating Work	Playing an Integer Game	150–151

Unit 10: Building and Filling

Launch	How can we describe and build boxes?	152–153
Activity 1	Boxes, Boxes, Boxes!	154
Activity 2	Bigger (and Better?) Boxes	155–156
Activity 3	Volumes: Change or No Change?	157–158
Activity 4	All Folded Up	159–160
Activity 5	Wrap It Up	161
	People, Society, and Mathematics:	
	Pack Them In	162–163
Culminating Work	Building a Box	164–165

Unit 11: Exploring Similar Figures

Launch	When are shapes similar?	166–167
Activity 1	Right Triangles	168–169
Activity 2	What's Your Angle?	170–171
	People, Society, and Mathematics:	
	Same Shape, Different Size	172–173
Activity 3	Similar Flags?	174–175
Activity 4	Going Around in Quadrilaterals	176–177
Culminating Work	Making a Class Mural	178–179

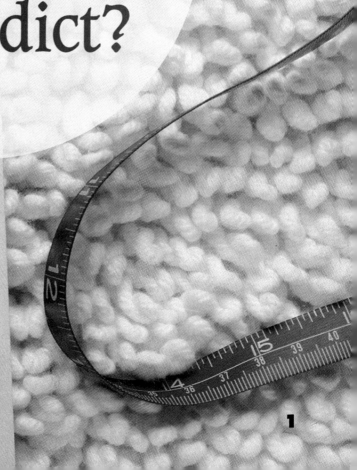

*H*ow can we use patterns to predict?

Time of Day	Temperature
10 a.m.	68°
12 p.m.	75°
7 a.m.	65°
3 p.m.	80°
6 p.m.	76°

Patterns Are Everywhere!

How can you describe the pattern that relates the height of the diving platform to the number of tiles needed in all?

Height of Diving Platform	Number of Tiles in All
2	5
3	6
4	?
5	?
6	?
7	?
•	•
•	•
•	•

Summer Olympics

▶ How can you describe the pattern that relates the number of gates to the number of tiles needed in all?

Number of Gates	Number of Tiles in all
1	5
2	10
3	15
4	?
•	•
•	•
•	•

Thebes, Egypt

GROWTH
PATTERNS
AND
RELATIONSHIPS

ON YOUR OWN

▶ Write a rule that tells how to find the output number when you know the input number. Use your rule to copy and complete the table.

1.

Input	Output
2	4
4	8
5	10
7	14
12	24
20	?
50	?

2.

Input	Output
10	3
15	8
20	13
25	18
30	23
35	?
40	?

3. Draw pictures of the next two designs. Write the rule in words. Use your rule to complete the table.

Number of gates	Number of tiles
1	6
2	12
3	18
4	?
5	?
6	?

4. Make up data for a T-table that follows a rule. Exchange with a classmate to find the rule.

5. *My Journal:* What have you learned about patterns and tables?

How Many Does It Take?

1. How many boxes should be on the bottom row to build a pyramid with 45 boxes?

Number in Bottom Row	Total Number of Boxes
1	1
2	3
3	6
4	?
•	•
•	•
•	•

2. A patio was designed like the one below. There are 50 tiles to be used. How many blocks should be placed in the middle row to use the greatest number of blocks?

Tiles in the Middle Row	Total Number of Tiles
1	1
2	4
3	9
4	?
•	•
•	•
•	•

CREATING,
ANALYZING,
AND EXTENDING
PATTERNS

5

ON YOUR OWN

1. The first three pentagonal numbers are listed and shown below. Copy and complete the table. How can you describe the pattern? Write a rule for the pattern.

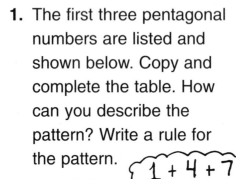
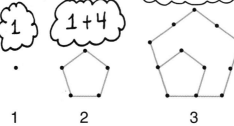

Design Number	Total Number of Dots
1	1
2	5
3	12
4	?
5	?
6	?
•	•
•	•
•	•

1 2 3

Hint: Draw the next two designs. How is each number sentence different from the one before?

2. The first three hexagonal numbers are listed and shown below. Copy and complete the table. How can you describe the pattern? Write a rule for the pattern.

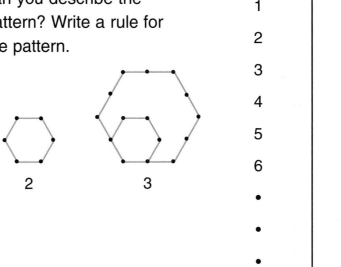

Design Number	Total Number of Dots
1	1
2	6
3	15
4	?
5	?
6	?
•	•
•	•
•	•

1 2 3

3. *My Journal:* Which pattern was most difficult for you to find? Explain why.

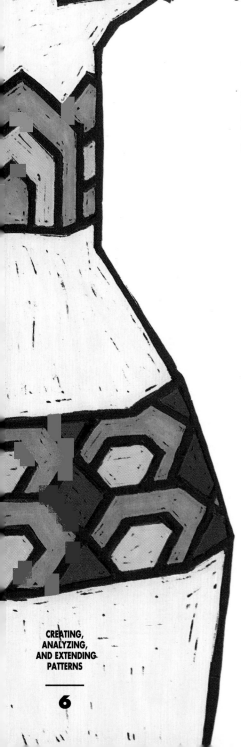

CREATING, ANALYZING, AND EXTENDING PATTERNS

Growing Designs

Describe the patterns you see in each table.
How many **triangles** are needed for Design Number 10?
How many **squares** are needed for Design Number 10?

Design Number	Number of Triangles	Design Number	Number of Squares
1	4	1	1
2	8	2	4
3	12	3	9
4	?	4	?
5	?	5	?
6	?	6	?
7	?	7	?
8	?	8	?
9	?	9	?
10	?	10	?

▶ Copy and complete each table
to help you find out.

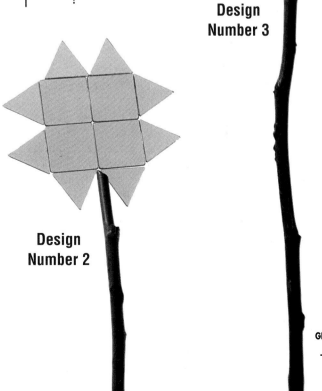

Design Number 3

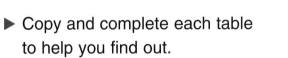

Design Number 2

Design Number 1

How do you plot points?

1 Quantity 1 is on the horizontal axis.
Quantity 2 is on the vertical axis.

Quantity 1	Quantity 2
1	2
2	3
3	4
4	5
5	6
6	7

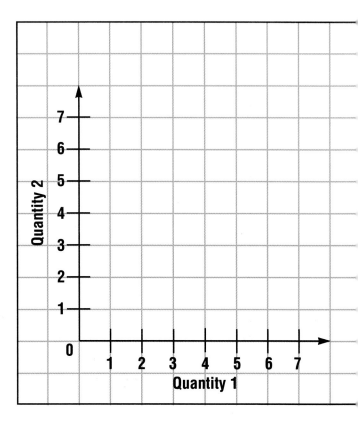

2 You can write or think about **ordered pairs** using a T-Table.

Quantity 1	Quantity 2		
1	2	→	(1,2)
2	3	→	(2,3)
3	4	→	(3,4)
4	5	→	(4,5)
5	6	→	(5,6)
6	7	→	(6,7)

These are ordered pairs.

Start at 0.

Go to the right two units.

(2,3)

Go up three units.

Quantity 2

7
6
5
4
3
2
1

0

1 2 3 4 5 6 7

Quantity 1

Quantity 2

7
6
5
4
3
2
1

0

1 2 3 4 5 6 7

Quantity 1

3 You can plot ordered pairs on a graph.

4 Look at the pattern formed when you plot the rest of the points.

It's easy.
Just follow the steps!

ON YOUR OWN

▶ Look at these designs. Copy and complete the T-table. Then use grid paper to be sure your graph is large enough to graph all the data. Graph the data.

Triangle Bridge

1. How many triangles would you need if you used 10 hexagons?

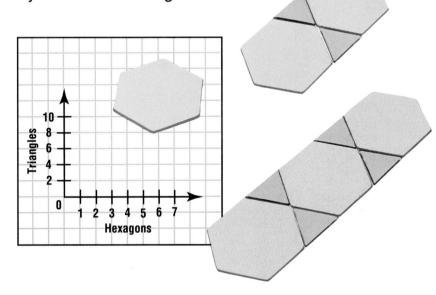

Hexagons	Triangles
1	0
2	2
3	4
4	?
5	?
6	?

Growing Flowers

2. How many tan pieces would you need if you had 12 blue pieces?

Blue Pieces	Tan Pieces
1	4
2	8
3	12
4	?
5	?
6	?

3. *My Journal:* What have you learned about coordinate graphing?

Do the Hand Squeeze!

▶ About how long do you think it would take the students in the picture to pass the hand squeeze?

**MEASURING
AND
PREDICTING**

11

ON YOUR OWN

1. Copy and complete the table below. Use grid paper to make a line graph for these data. Use the graph to predict the time for 25, 30, and 35 hand squeezes.

Number of hand squeezes	5	10	15	20	25	30	35
Time needed to make squeezes (in seconds)	4	8	12	16	?	?	?

2. What do you think would happen in the hand-squeezing experiment if you waited a week and tried it again? If you did it with your eyes closed?

3. *My Journal:* What are line graphs helpful to show? Explain.

AMAZING
F A C T S

You probably know that many deaf or hearing impaired people communicate with their hands by using sign language. But did you know that music can also be communicated through signing? Kathleen Taylor of New York signs for a variety of musical performances. Her signing allows many people to experience the joys of music.

Number Crunchers

► How is each Number Cruncher "crunching" the input?

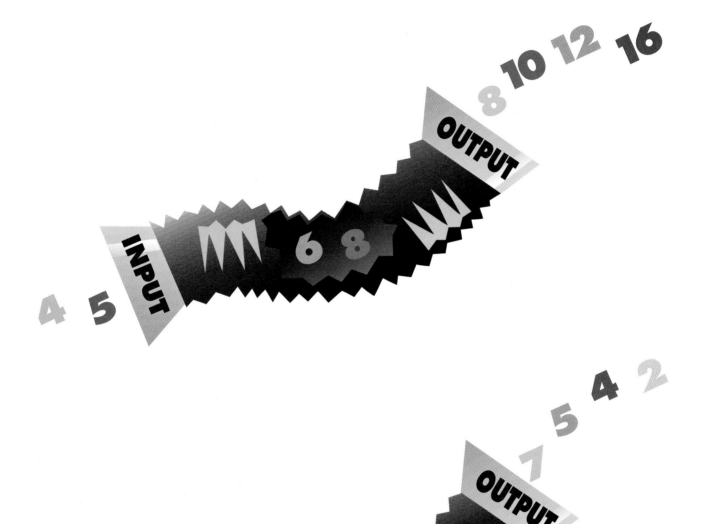

▶ Crunchers can also "crunch" polygons. How is each Cruncher "crunching" the input polygons?

1.

2.

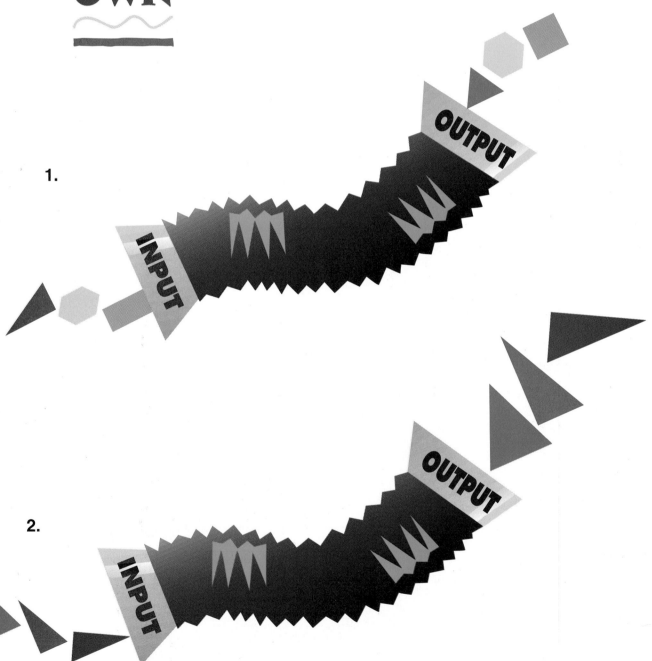

Rule:
Multiply first number
by 2. Add the second.

▶ What rule is used?

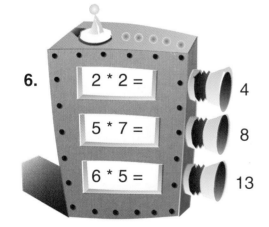

2 * 1 =   5

3 * 4 =   10

0 * 2 =   2

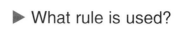

3.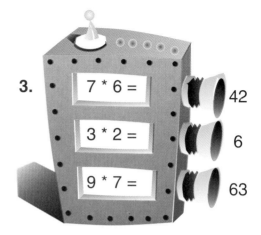

7 * 6 =   42

3 * 2 =   6

9 * 7 =   63

4.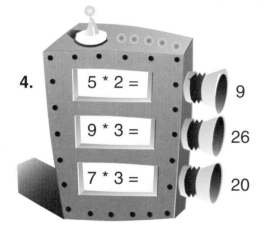

5 * 2 =   9

9 * 3 =   26

7 * 3 =   20

5.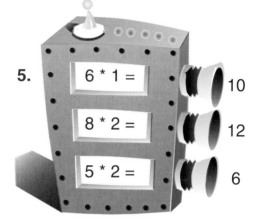

6 * 1 =   10

8 * 2 =   12

5 * 2 =   6

6.

2 * 2 =   4

5 * 7 =   8

6 * 5 =   13

7.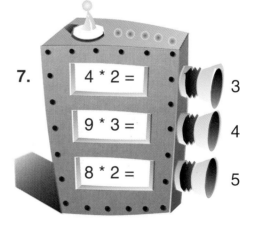

4 * 2 =   3

9 * 3 =   4

8 * 2 =   5

8. Make up your own rule. Write several examples using
your rule. See if someone else can find your rule.

9. *My Journal:* What have you learned about inputs,
patterns, and outputs?

Going Around in
CIRCLES, SQUARES,
and TRIANGLES

Have you ever wondered what number patterns people think are interesting, and why? Interest in mathematical patterns is not restricted to any one culture. People from China, Japan, Tibet, the Middle East, Africa, and elsewhere have experimented with number patterns. Some number patterns even take on geometric shapes.

Tibetan Number Square

Lo-Shu

Chinese Number Square

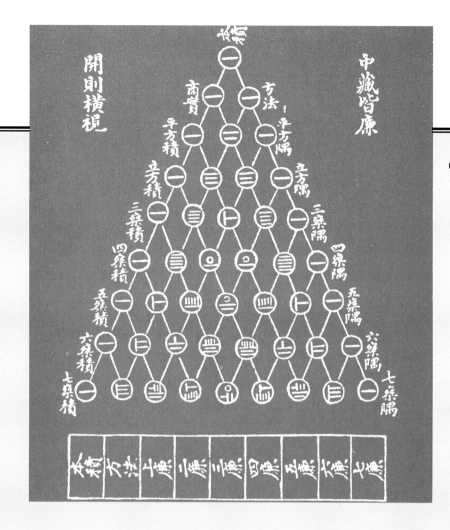

Chinese Triangle

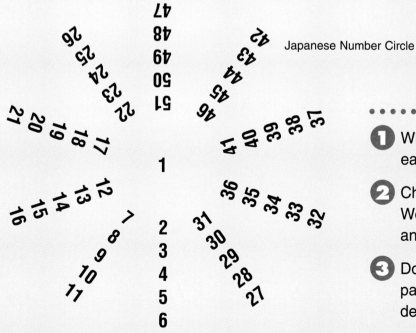

Japanese Number Circle

. . . .

1 What patterns do you see in each figure?

2 Choose one of the figures. Work with your group to find and describe the patterns.

3 Do you know any other number patterns? Can you find and describe one or create one?

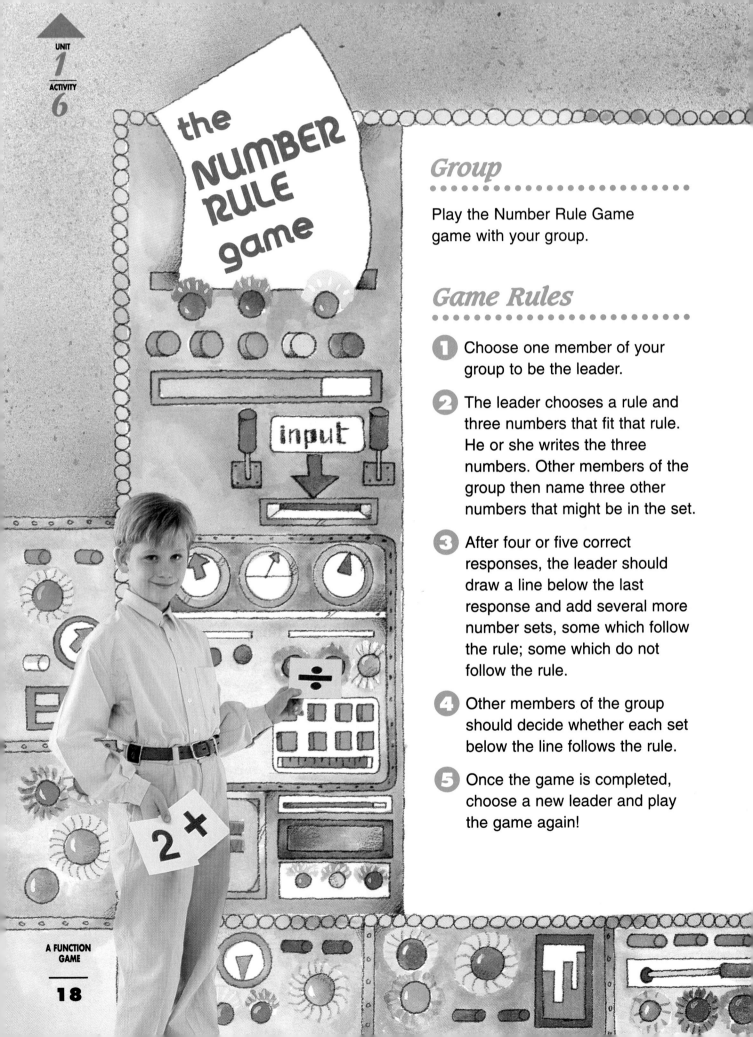

the NUMBER RULE game

input

2 +

Group

Play the Number Rule Game game with your group.

Game Rules

1 Choose one member of your group to be the leader.

2 The leader chooses a rule and three numbers that fit that rule. He or she writes the three numbers. Other members of the group then name three other numbers that might be in the set.

3 After four or five correct responses, the leader should draw a line below the last response and add several more number sets, some which follow the rule; some which do not follow the rule.

4 Other members of the group should decide whether each set below the line follows the rule.

5 Once the game is completed, choose a new leader and play the game again!

1. What's the rule for each set of data?

A

2	2	5
3	2	7
4	2	9
8	2	17
10	4	41

B

4	2	1
9	5	2
7	1	3
12	4	4
15	3	6

2. Which of these sets follow the rule for A?

3	5	9
6	2	12
1	0	1

3. Which of these sets follow the rule for B?

4	0	2
8	3	3
16	4	6

What's the Best Deal?

▶ What would you rather be paid: a million dollars for a month or a penny the first day, two pennies the second day, and so on, doubling the number of pennies each day for a month?

GET RICH QUICK!

$ $ $ $ $ $ $ $ $ $ $ $ $

Double Your Money Daily!

$ $ $ $ $ $ $ $ $ $ $ $.$

Start with only

1¢

September

		1	2	3	4
7	8	9	10	11	
14	15	Plant Tree! 16	17	18	
21	22	23	24	25	
28	29	30			

WIN A MILLION DOLLARS IN ONE MONTH!

BIG BUCKS DOLLAR DRIVE   123

PAY TO THE ORDER OF *Your Name Here!* $1,000,000

One Million Dollars 00/100

MAIL ¢

To Resident
1212 National Lane
Americaville, USA

1. Which would you rather earn: $100 for 15 days work or $1 the first day and $2 more each day you worked than the day before for 15 days?

2. Which bus would be less crowded: a bus with 45 passengers or a bus that has made 8 stops. At the first stop 1 person got on, at the second stop 2 people got on, at the third stop 3 people got on and so on.

3. Which choice would give you the most trees in your yard at the end of 5 years: planting 20 trees all at once or planting 2 trees the first year and then adding 3 trees per year after that?

4. Which situation would leave you with the most money saved at the end of 8 weeks: save $400 all at once or save $2 the first week and then double the amount saved each week after that? How much would you have?

5. *My Journal:* How were patterns helpful as you did this activity and the problems?

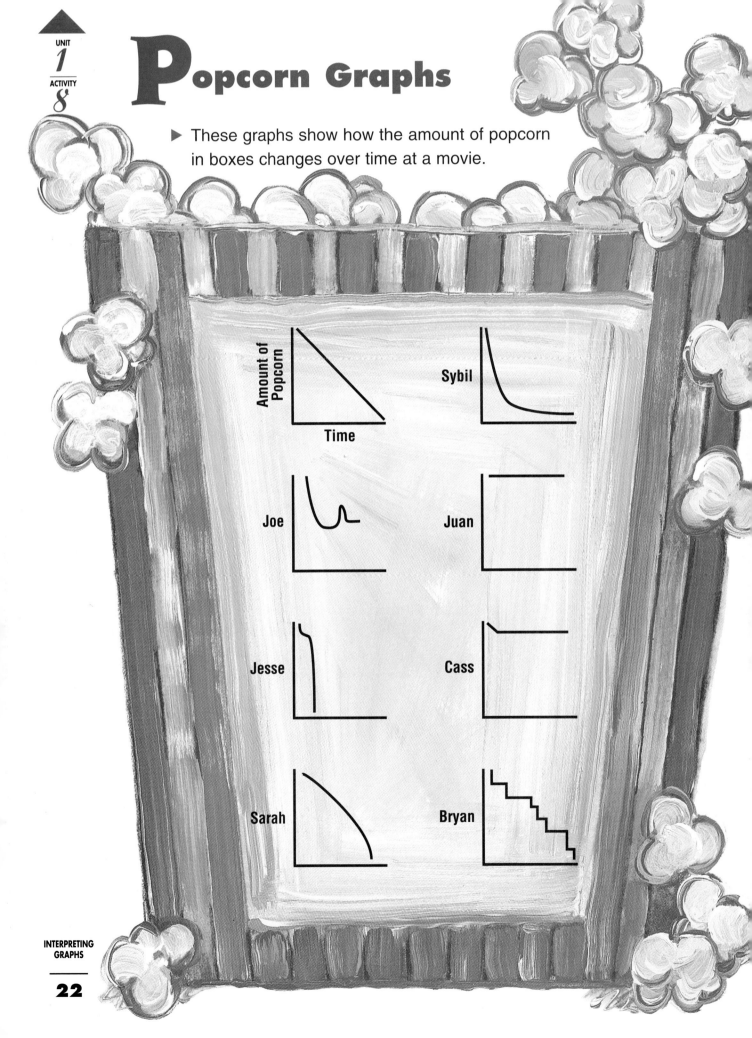

Popcorn Graphs

▶ These graphs show how the amount of popcorn in boxes changes over time at a movie.

▶ Which activity do you think goes with which graph?
Explain your reasoning.

a. Number of people watching television at a given time

b. Number of students doing schoolwork at a given time

c. Number of people at a shopping mall at a given time

d. Number of people eating a meal at a given time

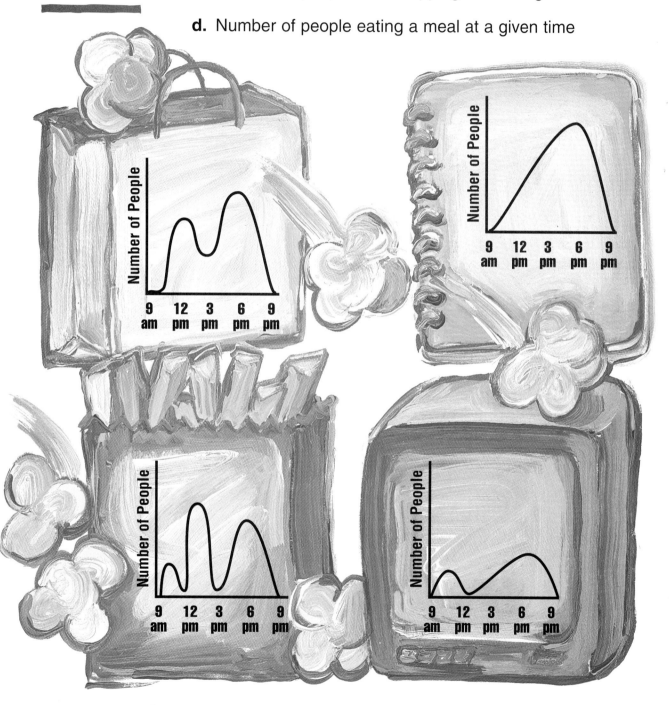

My Journal: How comfortable do you feel interpreting
graphs that show relationships? Explain.

Experimenting with a PENDULUM

One swing of a pendulum starts when the bob is at the far left. The swing is complete when the bob gets to the far right.

Here are two different ways to make a pendulum. What are the advantages and disadvantages of each?

Make a pendulum of your own. Then use it to do some experiments. For each experiment, create a data table, and record your results in a graph.

- How many times does the pendulum swing in 1 minute?

- How long does it take for one swing?

- Does the time change if you change the weight of the bob? the length of the string? the width of the swing?

- Create one experiment of your own. Decide what you are testing. Predict what will happen ahead of time. Then experiment to see if your prediction was correct!

Check YOURSELF

Great job! You made a pendulum and used it for some experiments. Your plans, data, and results were clearly written for each experiment. You used data tables and graphs to show your results. And, you wrote to explain how data tables and graphs were used in your experiments.

**Exploring
Tessellations**

*W*hat shapes cover completely?

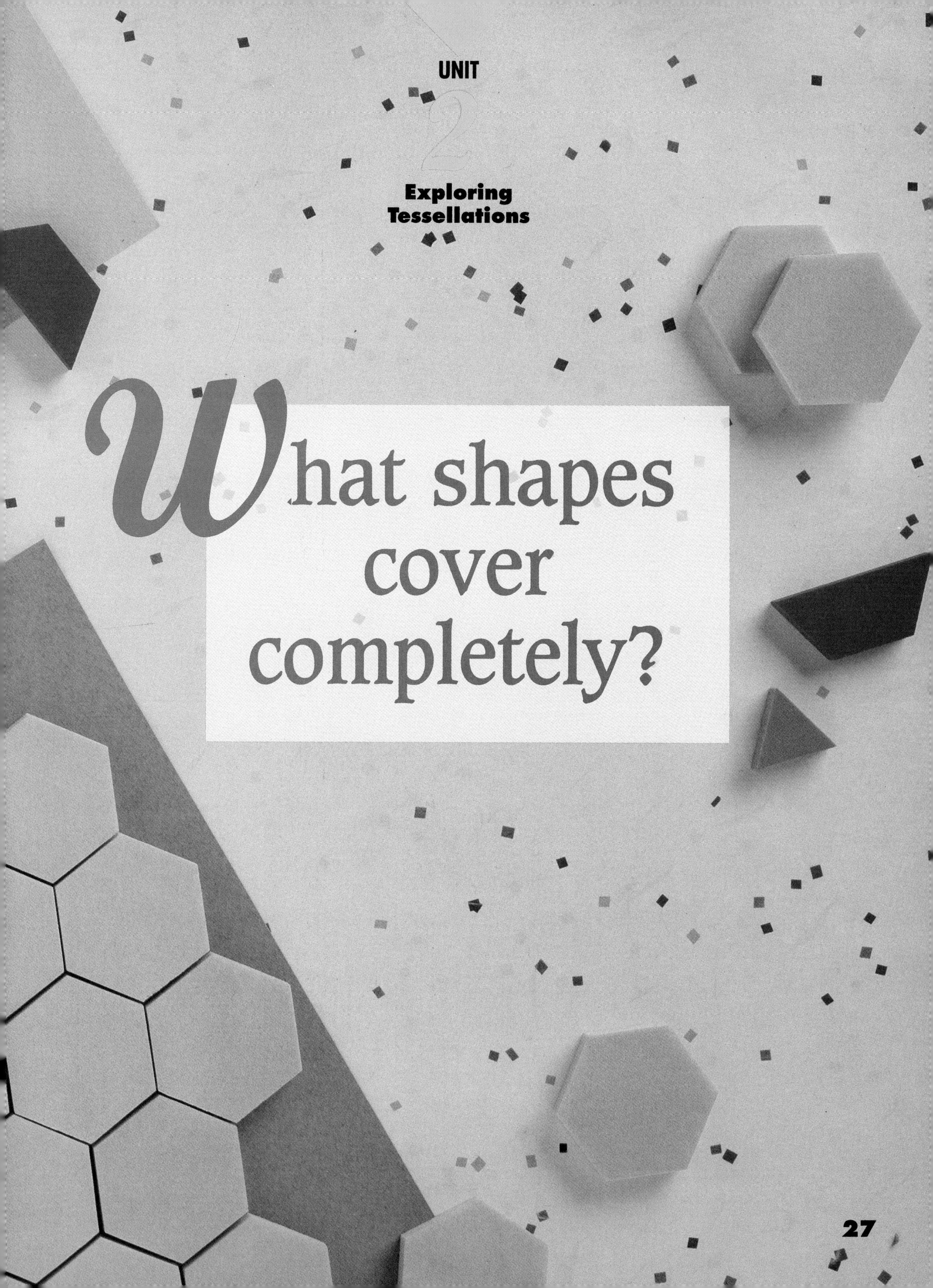

Any Designs On It?

▶ Discuss each design in your group.

Cover Ups!

A tessellation is an infinite set of shapes that covers
the whole plane. Tessellations are also called tilings.

▶ Which picture does not show
a tessellation?

A regular tessellation is made with just one regular polygon repeated over and over. All the tiles are congruent. These tessellations are edge-to-edge.

▶ What polygons do you see in each picture?

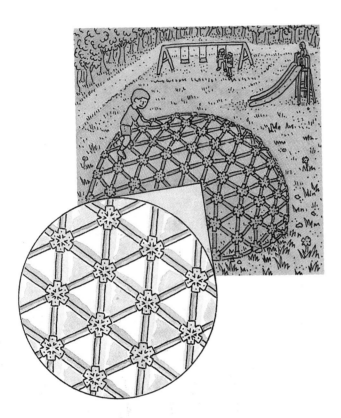

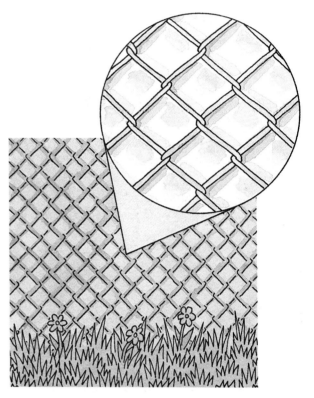

AMAZING
F A C T S

One of the largest office buildings in the world is the Pentagon Building. It's the headquarters of the Department of Defense of the United States government. The building is the shape of a regular pentagon and covers 29 acres.

The Latest In
HOME FASHIONS

Have you ever wondered where patterns for material in your home might come from? You could furnish your home in tessellations. First you might choose from a variety of Islamic tiling patterns for your floors.

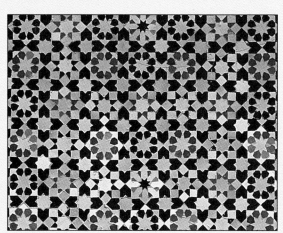

You might cover some of your floors with American Indian rug designs.

Some of your curtains might be made from African fabrics.

Now all you need is a colorful stained glass window.

1 Look for tessellating patterns in your home, school, or neighborhood. See if you can find out where they came from.

2 Use some polygons you like to make a tessellating pattern. Tell where you might like to use it in your home.

3 Do you prefer tessellating patterns or other kinds of patterns? Explain your choice.

Plane Covers

▶ Which polygons are used in these tessellations?
Are the polygons regular?

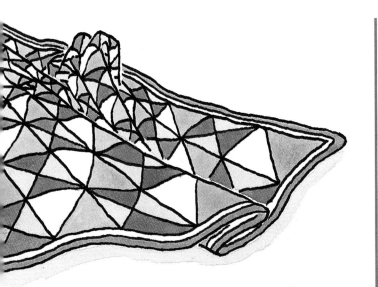

ON YOUR OWN

1. Describe the polygons you see in each picture.
Are they regular?

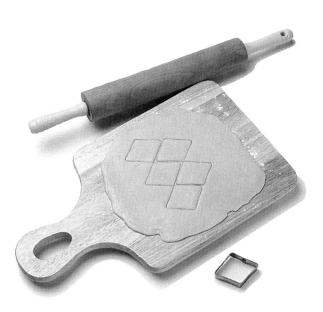

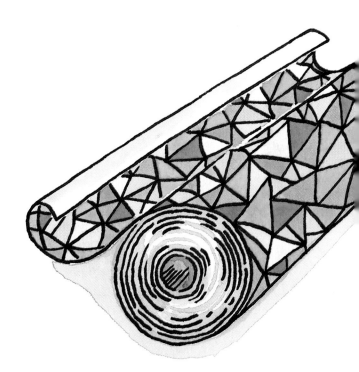

2. *My Journal:* What have you learned
about tessellations so far?

Tessellation Combinations

▶ Discuss each tessellation. Name the polygons.

▶ Write a brief description of each tessellation.

1.

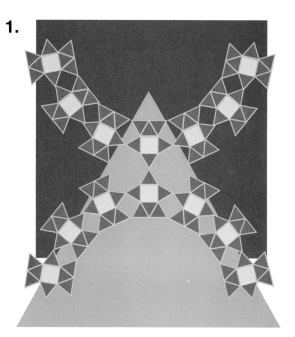

2.

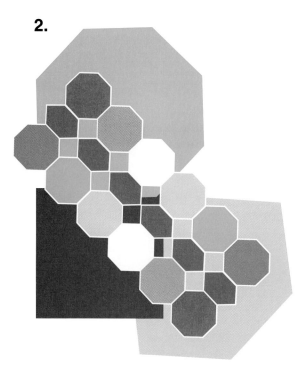

3.

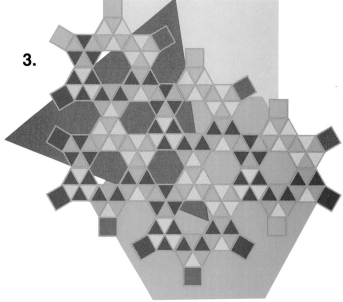

4.

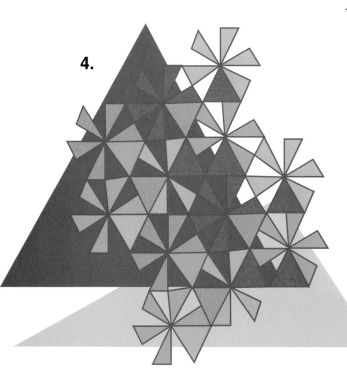

**5. *My Journal:* Is there anything about tessellations you do not understand? Explain your difficulties.

COMBINING
TWO OR MORE
REGULAR
POLYGONS

35

A PUZZLING PROBLEM

How are these puzzles alike?
How are they different?

36

Here is an example of a puzzle made from a tessellation pattern. Where are the lines of symmetry when the pieces are together?

Create a puzzle of your own using geometric shapes. Think about whether you want your puzzle to have lines of symmetry. Write to explain how you used tessellations and symmetry in your puzzle.

Check YOURSELF

Great job! You made a puzzle that used geometric shapes and colors in an interesting way. You explained clearly in writing how symmetry and tessellations were used in your puzzle.

How
can
we use
operations?

Pizza Party

▶ Use this menu to decide how many pizzas and soft drinks to order for a class party.

~PIZZAS~

Large   (8 slices) $12.95
Small   (4 slices) $9.75

Each Topping $0.25

Toppings
Sausages, Pepperoni, Mushroom, Onions, Olives, Green Pepper

~Soft Drinks~
6 Packs $2.99
Case (24 cans) $7.50

Sorry, no single cans or slices

ON YOUR OWN

► For each expression, write a story problem that might be solved by doing that calculation. Then solve the problem. Show all your work.

1. 3×28

2. $18 + 28 + 16$

3. $85 - 13$

4. $16 \div 4$

5. $2 \times (8 + 7)$

6. *My Journal:* What have you learned about choosing operations to solve a problem?

Peas Share!

I eat my peas with honey.
I've done it all my life.
It makes the peas taste funny.
But it keeps them on the knife.

Range Rover

▶ What number multiplied by 48 gives a product in the range between 250 and 325?

```
250                 Try 5.    48 × 5 = 240        250
 ┬                            Too small!           ┬
 │                                                 │
 │      48 × _?_    Try 6.    48 × 6 = 288        288
 │                            OK!                   │
 ┴                                                  ┴
325                                                325
```

▶ Find each missing number.

1.
$$53 \times \underline{\ ?\ } \quad \text{Range:} \quad \begin{array}{c} 340 \\ \hline \\ \hline 400 \end{array}$$

4.
$$25 \times \underline{\ ?\ } \quad \text{Range:} \quad \begin{array}{c} 1{,}130 \\ \hline \\ \hline 1{,}170 \end{array}$$

2.
$$37 \times \underline{\ ?\ } \quad \text{Range:} \quad \begin{array}{c} 130 \\ \hline \\ \hline 160 \end{array}$$

5.
$$59 \times \underline{\ ?\ } \quad \text{Range:} \quad \begin{array}{c} 4{,}550 \\ \hline \\ \hline 4{,}650 \end{array}$$

3.
$$14 \times \underline{\ ?\ } \quad \text{Range:} \quad \begin{array}{c} 440 \\ \hline \\ \hline 460 \end{array}$$

6.
$$62 \times \underline{\ ?\ } \quad \text{Range:} \quad \begin{array}{c} 5{,}100 \\ \hline \\ \hline 5{,}200 \end{array}$$

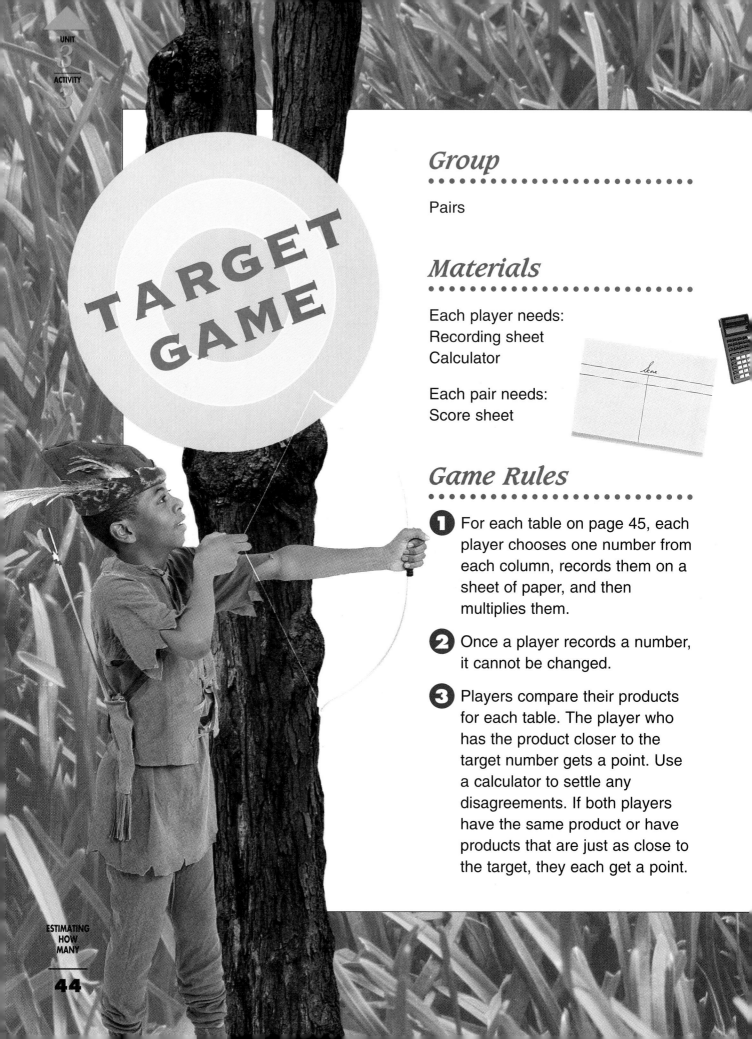

TARGET GAME

Group

Pairs

Materials

Each player needs:
Recording sheet
Calculator

Each pair needs:
Score sheet

Game Rules

1 For each table on page 45, each player chooses one number from each column, records them on a sheet of paper, and then multiplies them.

2 Once a player records a number, it cannot be changed.

3 Players compare their products for each table. The player who has the product closer to the target number gets a point. Use a calculator to settle any disagreements. If both players have the same product or have products that are just as close to the target, they each get a point.

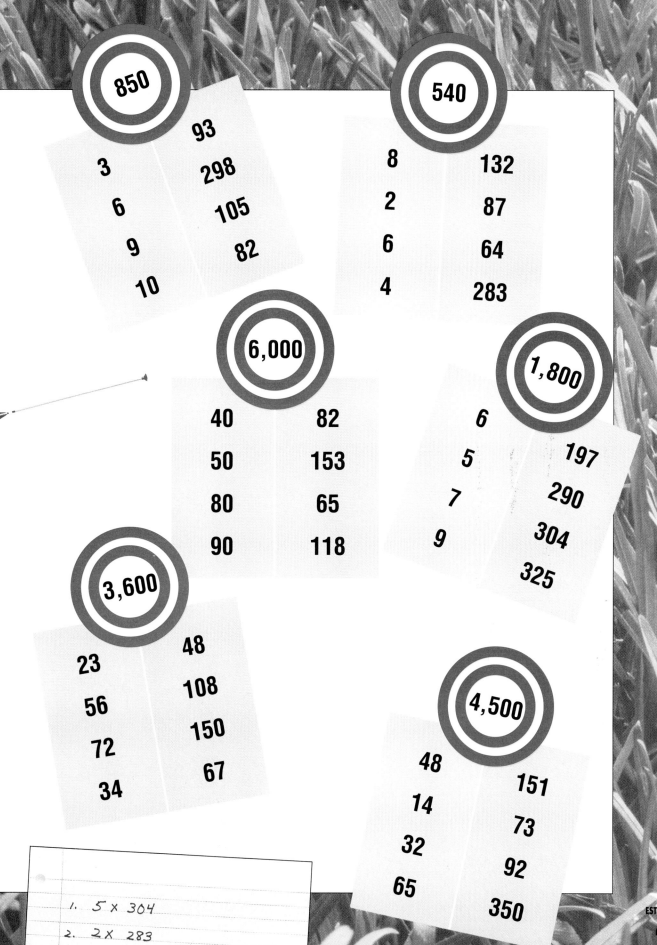

850
93
3   298
6   105
9   82
10

540
8   132
2   87
6   64
4   283

6,000
40   82
50   153
80   65
90   118

1,800
6   197
5   290
7   304
9   325

3,600
23   48
56   108
72   150
34   67

4,500
48   151
14   73
32   92
65   350

1. 5 × 304
2. 2 × 283

The Great Divide

▶ How did this student find 75 ÷ 6?

Chalkboard Talk

$75 \div 6$

$6+6+6+6+6+6$

$6+6+6+6+6+6$

60
12   72

12 sixes and
3 left over.

▶ Divide using your own procedures. Be prepared to explain your procedures.

1 54 ÷ 5

2 126 ÷ 8

3 88 ÷ 12

4 145 ÷ 25

5 Make up a division expression and find the quotient.

6 How do you check your work?

164 ÷ 7 = 23 and 3 left over. Is this correct?

AMAZING
F A C T S

In North America, one of the first printed examples of a procedure to do division was found in Sumario Compendioso *by Juan Diez in the early 16th century. For the problem 114,400 ÷ 26 = 4,400 it looked like this:*

OO
12
0300
114400/4400
26666
222

Yodos, Modos and Hodos

▶ Yodos, Modos, and Hodos like to play Boboball, a version of soccer known only to inhabitants of outer space. All three groups must play in a game, but the number on each team and the total number of players can change for each game.

Find how many Yodos, Modos, and Hodos are in each game.

1. There are 2 Yodos.
There are twice as many Hodos as Yodos.
There are 55 players in all.

2. There are 48 Modos.
There are 12 fewer Hodos than Modos.
There are 102 players in all.

3. There are 8 Modos.
There are 3 times as many Hodos as Modos.
There are 60 in all.

4. There are 12 Yodos.
There are twice as many Modos as Hodos.
There are 60 players in all.

5. There are 30 Modos.
There are half as many Hodos as Yodos.
There are 78 players in all.

ON YOUR OWN

▶ Find how many Yodos, Modos, and Hodos are in each game.

1. There are 20 Hodos.
There are 8 fewer Modos than Hodos.
There are 82 players in all.

2. There are 15 Yodos.
There are 10 more Hodos than Modos.
There are 75 players in all.

3. There are 35 Modos.
There are twice as many Yodos as Hodos.
There are 80 players in all.

4. Make up a problem about 50 Yodos, Modos, and Hodos in a game. Trade problems with a classmate and solve.

5. *My Journal:* Which problem about Yodos, Modos, and Hodos was easiest for you to solve? Why? Which problem about Yodos, Modos, and Hodos was the most difficult for you to solve? Why?

Front Seats and Back Seats

▶ You need to buy 26 tickets for a sports event.
You have $348 and must spend it all. What type tickets
can you buy? How many of each type can you buy?

▶ Suppose you had $348 to buy 26 tickets.
This time you can spend all the money
on tickets or save part of it to use for
another activity. What combination(s) of
back and front seats could you buy that
would cost less than $348? How can you
save the most money?

Baseball
Game

fRONt $18
Back $12

Back
fRont

Eight-Year-Old

CARL

PEOPLE,
SOCIETY, AND
MATHEMATICS

Have you ever wondered how people developed efficient ways to work with numbers? When Carl Friedrich Gauss, the German mathematician and founder of number theory, was about eight years old, his teacher asked the class to find the sum of all the whole numbers from 1 to 100. It seemed like a task that would take a long time. Within seconds, Carl had the answer.

He used mental math strategies and multiplication. First he recognized that pairing the numbers would help.

Although we do not know their names, people in other parts of the world developed efficient systems, too. The people of Nigeria used the Yoruba numbers for large quantities. The Yoruba system had 14 numbers: 1 to 10, 20, 30, 200, and 400. All other numbers were formed by adding, subtracting, or multiplying.

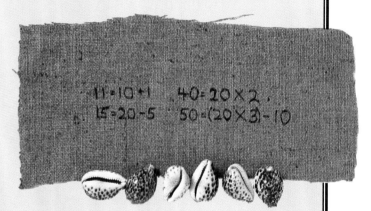

$$11 = 10 + 1 \qquad 40 = 20 \times 2$$
$$15 = 20 - 5 \qquad 50 = (20 \times 3) - 10$$

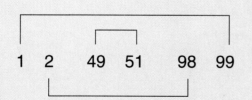

He got 49 sums of 100 or 49 x 100 = 4,900. By adding 50 and 100, the numbers that were not paired, he got the total of 5,050.

❶ Calculate the sum of all the numbers from 1 up to but not including 10 Carl's way. Then do it the long way. Do you get the same number?

❷ Calculate the sum of all the numbers from 1 up to 500.

❸ Represent 28 and 42 in the Yoruba system.

51

Jiminy Cricket!

▶ What is the total length of this cricket's jumps?

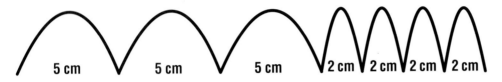

5 cm   5 cm   5 cm   2 cm 2 cm 2 cm 2 cm

▶ **Jump Rules**

In each problem, big jumps are the same length and little jumps are the same length. Jumps in different problems may be different lengths. Big jumps are longer than little jumps, and all jumps are a whole number of units long.

How long is each jump?

1. Total length: 24 in.

2. Total length: 24 cm

3. Total length: 16 in.

4. Total length: 26 cm

5. Total length: 28 cm

ON YOUR OWN

▶ Solve these problems.
Use the same rules as on page 52.

1. Total length: 22 centimeters. How long is each little jump?

5 cm   5 cm   ?   ?   ?

2. Total length: 25 centimeters. How long is each big jump?

?   ?   ?   2 cm   2 cm

3. Total length: 50 centimeters. How long is each jump?

▶ Write a problem for each set of cricket jumps. Then exchange your problems with a classmate and solve.

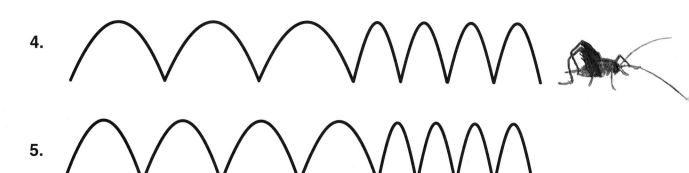

4.

5.

6. *My Journal:* Which of the problems on this page was easiest to solve? Why? Which problem was most difficult? Why?

Name that Number!

▶ Solve these puzzles.

1. I am a number.

Multiply me by 2.

Subtract 15 from the product.

You end with 21.

What number am I?

2. I am a number.

Add 25 to me.

Divide the sum by 2.

You end with 75.

What number am I?

4. I am a number.

Add 4 times me to 25.

This sum is equal to 35 added to 2 times me.

What number am I?

3. I am a number.

Add me to 16.

Multiply the sum by 5.

The product is equal to 6 times me.

What number am I?

AND THE NUMBER IS...

SOLVING
PROBLEMS USING
LOGIC AND
OPERATION
SENSE

54

What Numbers Are We?

▶ Solve these puzzles.

1. We are two numbers.

   If you subtract one of us
   from the other, you get 6.

   If you add us, you get 30.

   What numbers are we?

2. We are two numbers.

   If you multiply
   our product
   by 2, you
   get 60.

   The difference
   between us is 1.

   What numbers
   are we?

3. We are two numbers.

   If you divide our
   sum by 2, you
   get 25.

   If you add 10 to one
   of us, you get the other
   one of us.

   What numbers are we?

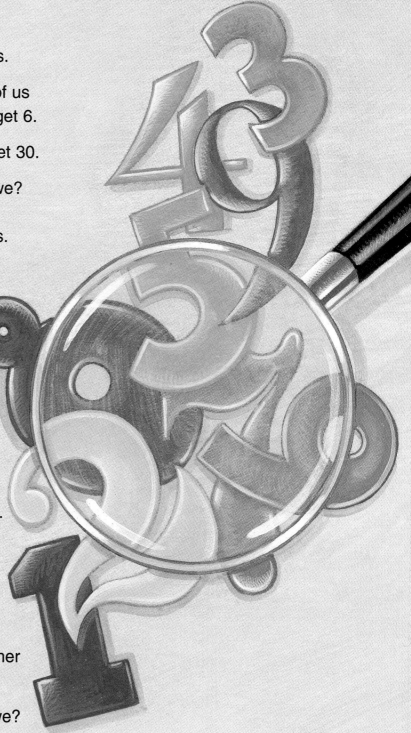

SOLVING
MORE PROBLEMS
USING
ALGEBRA

FUN FUND RAISING!

What are some things you could do to raise money? Have you ever helped raise money by doing any of these kinds of activities? What project were you raising the money for?

Car Wash
Cars $3.00

WIN A TV!

Raffle Tickets $2.00

TV Raffle

$2.00

$2.00

Design a complete plan for raising the funds for whatever your class decided on. Then write a report describing your plan and your work. Here are some things to think about.

- What should you consider when deciding how to raise funds?
- What expenses will you have?
- Will you sell tickets, a service, or an item?
- How much will you charge?
- How much money do you expect to raise?
- Is it possible that you could lose money? If so, how?
- How long will your fund-raising event last?

Check **Y**OURSELF

Great job! Your plan and report include all important information about the fund-raising event. Your report explains clearly how you did your work and shows an understanding of using appropriate operations and personal strategies for computation. Your plan and report were clear and easy to follow.

How can we show and use fractions?

From Finish to Start

▶ It's party time.

"Person 1 take one prize and $\frac{1}{3}$ of what is left. Pass on to person 2."

"Take one prize and $\frac{1}{3}$ of what is left. Pass on to person 3."

"Take one prize and $\frac{1}{3}$ of what is left. Pass on to person 4."

How many prizes were in the grab-bag to start with?

ON YOUR OWN

1. Plan a party. You have a box of 24 invitations. You will write 6 of the invitations yourself and 3 friends will share writing the remaining invitations equally. What fraction of the total number of invitations will each friend write?

2. You have enough money to buy 16 blueberry bubble gum bagels to share with your lucky guests and yourself. How many guests is it possible for you to invite so that each person gets the same number of bagels and there are none left over? How many guests do you think will want blueberry bubble gum bagels?

3. Your guests who have dogs can bring them to the party. You will, of course, have a box of canned food for the dogs. Beau gets $\frac{1}{4}$ of the cans, Woody gets $\frac{1}{3}$ of what is left. Trouble gets $\frac{1}{2}$ of what remains after that. Dot and Spot belong to the same guest and get the last remaining 13 cans together. How many cans of dog food were in the box at the beginning?

4. *My Journal:* What was the most difficult silly problem to solve? Explain why.

EXPLORING
FRACTIONS

61

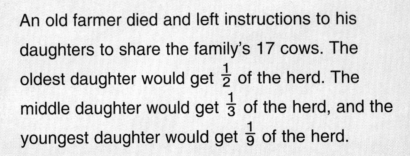

How Now, Brown Cow?

An old farmer died and left instructions to his daughters to share the family's 17 cows. The oldest daughter would get $\frac{1}{2}$ of the herd. The middle daughter would get $\frac{1}{3}$ of the herd, and the youngest daughter would get $\frac{1}{9}$ of the herd.

"How can this be?" cried the oldest daughter. "My share would be $8\frac{1}{2}$ cows!"

"Surely Father didn't want us to split our cows into pieces!" said the middle daughter.

"But how else can we obey Father's last wish?" asked the youngest daughter.

A passing stranger overheard the conversation. "Don't worry," she said. "Just take my brown cow and your problem will be over."

The daughters tried to talk the woman out of this unexpected gift, but she insisted. She added her cow to their herd, and watched and waited. The three daughters easily divided the herd according to their father's wishes. To their great surprise, after each took her share, there was one cow left—which they quickly returned to the stranger.

"It's a miracle! Thank you!" they cried. And the stranger left with her cow. How did this problem work out?

▶ Solve these problems. Show all your work.

1. You have 6 coins— $\frac{1}{2}$ are quarters, $\frac{1}{6}$ are dimes, and the rest are pennies. Draw a picture of your money. How much money do you have? What fraction of a dollar is this?

2. Of the 50 states in the United States $\frac{3}{10}$ of them have shorelines that border the Atlantic Ocean, $\frac{1}{10}$ of them have Pacific shorelines, and $\frac{1}{10}$ have Gulf of Mexico shorelines. How many states have each of type of shoreline? Can you name the states for each region?

3. The Statue of Liberty is 151 feet tall, from her feet to the tip of her torch. The length of her right arm, which holds the torch, is about $\frac{1}{4}$ of her total height. Give a reasonable estimate for that length. Explain how you got your answer.

4. The Wheeling Park High School Marching Band of West Virginia made the longest musical march on record. In October, 1989, the band marched $42\frac{1}{2}$ miles in just under 15 hours! Sixty-nine musicians started the march, but only about $\frac{1}{3}$ finished. About how many musicians finished the march that day?

5. *My Journal:* Which problem was easiest for you? Which was the most difficult? Explain.

Let's Go on a Fraction Hunt

▶ How many equivalent fractions can you find using Fraction Circles?

▶ How many equivalent fractions can you find using 24 counters?

ON YOUR OWN

1. Check on it. You receive a birthday check for $12.80. It is written with the fraction $\frac{80}{100}$. You know $\frac{80}{100}$ is not the simplest fraction. Should you ask the person who wrote you the check to use the equivalent fraction $\frac{4}{5}$? Explain.

2. Is it always best to write fractions using the smallest number possible? Explain.

3. *My Journal:* What did you learn that was new to you? Explain.

A Typical Day in the Life of Otto Upside Down

▶ What's wrong with these pictures?

1. Make a circle graph to show the typical day of a house pet, such as a cat, a dog, or a turtle.

2. Look at the pictures below. How many equivalent fractions or mixed numbers can you write for each situation?

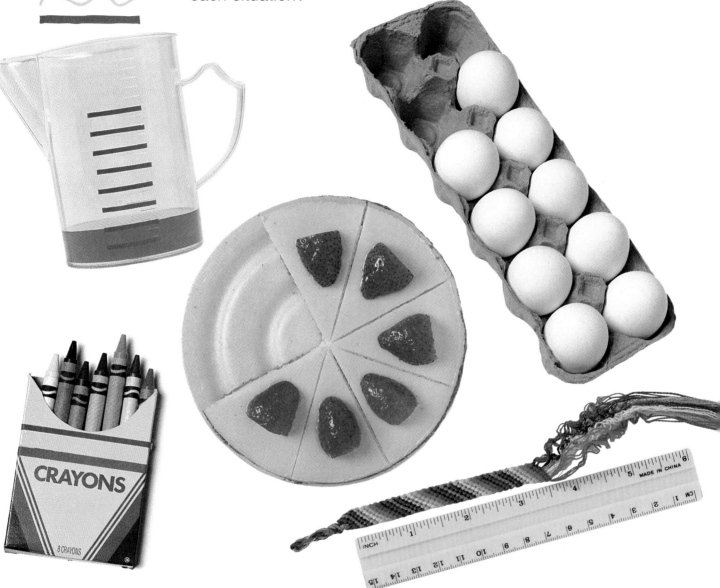

3. Describe several different situations in which you would rather use a fraction that is not in simplest form. Explain why you think it would be better to use a fraction that is not in simplest form in these situations.

4. *My Journal:* Is there anything about equivalent fractions that you still don't understand? Explain.

EQUIVALENT
FRACTIONS

Lots of Links

A welder is making a special chain for a hanging lamp.
She follows a pattern that alternates two different-sized links.

ON YOUR OWN

▶ Solve these problems.

1. How many links would the welder need for a 5-foot chain using only $1\frac{1}{2}$-inch links? How can you figure this out?

2. The welder cannot use the same special-chain pattern to make a chain exactly one foot long. Why? She could use same size links to reach exactly one foot. Draw and label your solution.

3. Suppose you ask for a necklace made from a lighter-weight version of the same two lengths of links. You want the necklace to be long enough to slip over your head, and you want to have more short links than long links. Determine a reasonable length for the necklace, draw its link pattern, and find the exact length as you have designed it.

4. Make up several fraction or mixed number problems so that the sum is between 2 and 3.

5. *My Journal:* What did you learn about combining fractions and mixed numbers? What would you still like to learn?

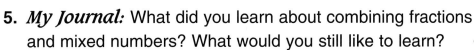

Fractions of TIME

Have you ever wondered how people who used different number systems expressed parts of wholes?

You know that you can express a part of a whole as a fraction or in a base ten system as a decimal. The Babylonians and the Alexandrians used a number system based on 60. The number 60 was useful as the year was considered to have 6 times 60 days.

The Greek astronomers developed their fraction system on the Babylonian base 60 system. The number 60 has many factors so it was easy to represent parts of 60. Because 60 has factors of 2, 3, 4, 5, 6, 10, 12, 15, 20 and 30 fractions such $\frac{1}{2}$, $\frac{1}{3}$, $\frac{1}{4}$, $\frac{1}{5}$, $\frac{1}{6}$, $\frac{1}{10}$, $\frac{1}{12}$, $\frac{1}{15}$, $\frac{1}{20}$, and $\frac{1}{30}$ were easily developed.

The notation for these fractions was, however, very different from the fraction notation used today.

1 What system based on 60 do you use every day? Think of how the Babylonians came to use 60.

2 What notation is used for this system? How would you represent $\frac{1}{2}$ hour? $\frac{1}{4}$ hour?

3 Draw a clock and show $\frac{1}{2}$ hour, $\frac{1}{4}$ hour, $\frac{3}{4}$ hour and other fractional parts of hours of your choice.

4 How does a digital clock show the same times as as an analog clock?

5 Explain how the same clock can be used to tell hours, minutes, and seconds.

6 Invent a system for showing parts of wholes.

Model Trains, Model Fractions

▶ What is the longest 2-car train you can make?

$2\frac{1}{8}$ in.   3 in. $2\frac{3}{4}$ in. $2\frac{7}{8}$ in.

▶ What is the shortest 2-car train you can make?

▶ What are all the different lengths you can make for a train using one engine and one or more other cars?

$2\frac{1}{8}$ in.

$1\frac{3}{4}$ in.

$2\frac{1}{2}$ in.

3 in.

$2\frac{7}{8}$ in.

$1\frac{1}{4}$ in.

AMAZING
F A C T S

Jean Damery of France built the smallest known working model railroad. His engine was only $\frac{5}{16}$ of an inch long. Based on a scale of 1:1,000 this would represent a real engine about 26 feet long.

ADDING AND SUBTRACTING FRACTIONS AND MIXED NUMBERS

Keep on SLIDING

What do the ramps shown have in common? How are they different? Why?

Now design and carry out this experiment: Make a simple ramp of wood or cardboard so that you can adjust its tilt and then measure and record its height from the floor in fractions of an inch. Measure how far a penny slides away from the bottom of the ramp for different tilts.

Make a graph to help show your results. Include answers to questions like these when you write about your experiment.

- What does the data prove about the relationship between the height of the ramp and the distance the penny slides? How does the data match what you expected to find? Explain.

- What is the combined distance of the two best slides? Did these "bests" come when you would have expected them? Explain.

- How much greater was the distance of the best slide than the worst slide? than the second best slide?

- How can you explain your worst slide?

- If you were going to try an experiment like this again, what would you do differently? Why?

- How did you use fractions in this project?

Check YOURSELF

Great job! You created a ramp with a height you can change, then used it to conduct the sliding experiment. You recorded the data accurately and chose a good graph to show it. You used your data to draw conclusions and make some predictions. You explained clearly in writing how fractional measurements were used in your experiment.

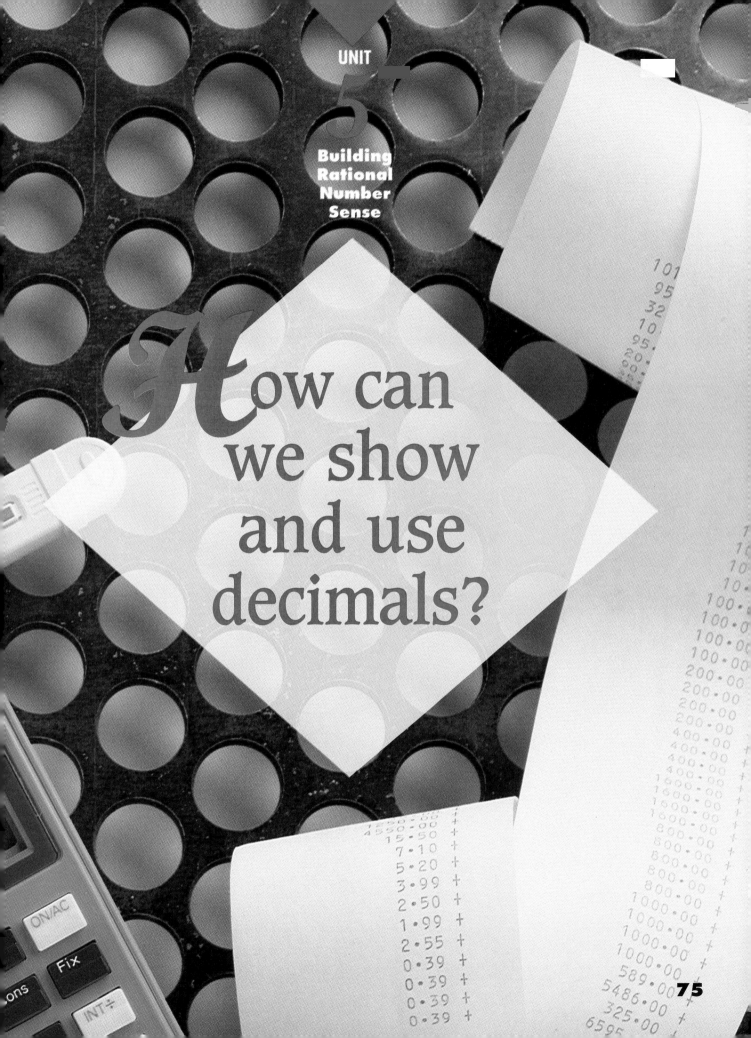

UNIT **5**

Building Rational Number Sense

How can we show and use decimals?

75

Tenths Around Us

▶ Write the decimal for each letter.

1.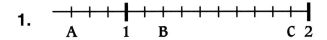

A   1   B   C 2

2.

6 D   E   F   7

3.

3   G   H   4   I   5

▶ Trace each part of a number line on your paper. Estimate to find and label the decimal.

4. Find 0.6.

0   0.2

5. Find 3.

0   0.5

6. Find 2.8.

0   0.7

7. Name three intervals on the number line that are 0.6 apart.

8. Name two intervals on the number line that are the same distance apart as 3.2 and 4.4.

9. *My Journal:* What do you know about how decimals are related to fractions?

The Decimal Place Value Game

Group

2 players

Materials

2 Game boards

_____ _____ • _____ _____ _____ _____

Each pair needs:

Number cards, 0–9
Two round counters or pennies
Score sheet

SCORE
David | Lien
III | II

Game Rules

Game 1
Goal: Build a decimal closer to 1.

1 You and your partner each put a counter on the table to serve as a decimal point.

2 One of you shuffles the cards and places them facedown in a stack in the center of the table.

3 The other draws the top card from the stack and lays it down directly to the left of the counter or in one of three places to the right of the counter. Once a card is down, you cannot move it.

4 Take turns drawing and laying down cards. Continue until each has had four turns. Whoever made the number closer to 1 scores a point.

5 Continue playing for five rounds, taking turns mixing the cards and starting each round.

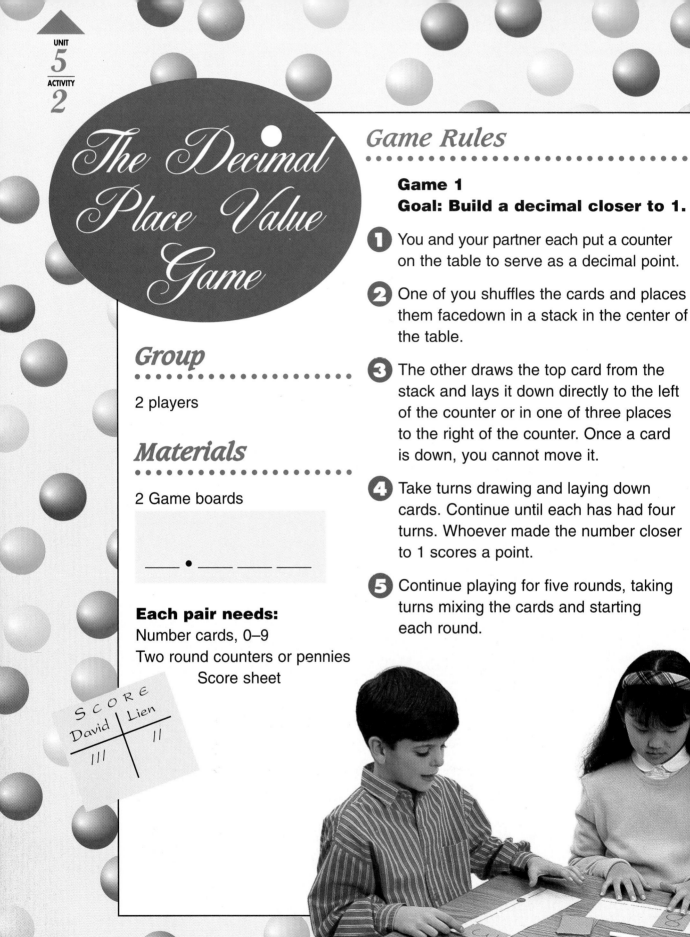

Game 2
Goal: Make the smaller number.

Follow the rules for GAME 1 with this new goal.

Game 3
Goal: Make the larger number.

Follow the rules for GAME 1 with this new goal.

Example: Game 3

	David	Lien
Turn 1	• 3	•8
Turn 2	2• 3	•8 7
Turn 3	2• 9 3	•8 7 5
Turn 4	2•0 9 3	6•8 7 5

Who won?

▶ One way to vary the Place Value Game is to switch the place of any two cards after four cards have been laid down. Solve these problems by doing this switch if you can.

1. Suppose you made the decimal 1.297. How many numbers greater than 1.297 can you make by switching two digits? Show them.

2. Suppose you made the decimal 3.405. How many numbers less than 3.405 can you make by switching two digits? Show them.

3. Make up your own variation of the Decimal Place Value Game. Change the rules any way you wish. Then play your variation with a classmate, friend, or family member.

4. *My Journal:* Do you know when one decimal is greater than another? Use examples to illustrate your explanation.

Eating Out

How many different lunches could you order from this menu for $7.50 or less?

ZEBRA DINER!

SOUPS AND SALADS

tomato soup — 1.95
black bean soup — 2.25
taco salad — 3.25
tuna salad — 2.95
chef's salad — 3.99
small green salad — 1.75

SANDWICHES

turkey — 4.35
ham and cheese — 5.95
bean burrito — 2.99
chicken burrito — 3.59
hamburger — 3.79
cheeseburger — 4.39
grilled chicken — 4.75

HOT DISHES

beef chili — 5.95
macaroni and cheese — 4.59
chimichanga — 5.75
franks and beans — 3.89
veal parmigiana — 5.95

BEVERAGES AND DESSERTS

pie — 1.95
fruit salad — 1.49
ice cream sundae — 3.59
milk/chocolate milk — 1.25
juices — 1.45

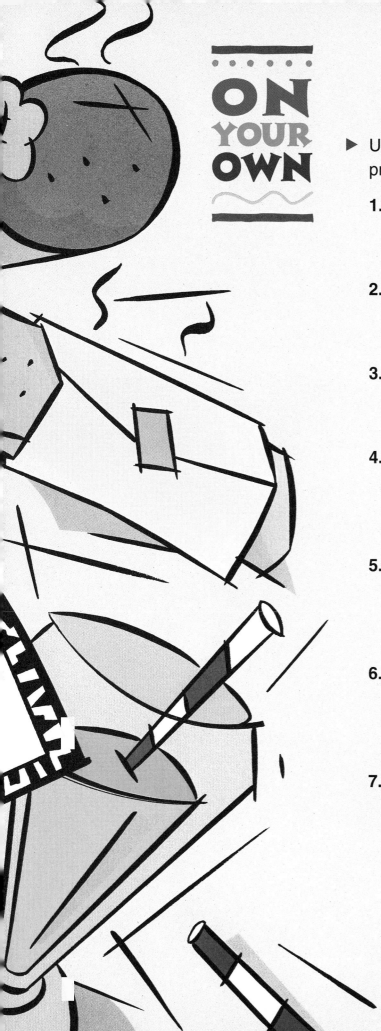

ON YOUR OWN

▶ Use the menu on page 80 for these problems.

1. Which items would you order for lunch if you were on a low fat diet? What is their total cost?

2. Which items would you order for lunch if you were allergic to dairy products? What is their total cost?

3. Which items would you order for lunch if you were a vegetarian? What is their total cost?

4. Suppose you were treating a friend to lunch. You had $15. What would the two of you order? What is the total cost of lunch?

5. Suppose your family went out to lunch to celebrate your birthday. What would each person order? What would be the total cost of lunch?

6. Make up a problem about ordering lunch from the menu on page 80. Exchange problems with a classmate and solve.

7. *My Journal:* What have you learned about adding decimals?

More Money

▶ Work with your partner to solve these problems.

1. If you have $1.50 to spend on pretzels, how many pretzels can you get if you spend all of your money?

Soft pretzels $.25 each. Buy 3 get 1 free.

2. Buy a battery. Use ten coins. What coins will you use?

Batteries $.73 each

3. You have $3.70 in dimes and quarters. You have nine more dimes than quarters. How many quarters do you have?

4. Suppose you were asked to shovel snow every day it snowed one winter. You agreed on pay of $.01 for the first day, $.02 for the second day, $.04 the third day, $.08 the fourth day, and so on. You work 13 days that winter. How much will you be paid on the thirteenth day? How much will you be paid altogether?

5. You have $52 to buy tickets for the community play. Adult tickets are $7.50 each and student tickets are $4.75 each. If you buy eight tickets and get $.25 change, how many of each type ticket did you buy?

ON YOUR OWN

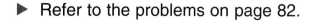

▶ Refer to the problems on page 82.

1. Refer to problem 1 to answer these problems.

   a. How much would it cost to get 2 pretzels? 5 pretzels?

   b. What plan could you follow to find the cost of any number of pretzels?

2. Refer to problem 2 to answer these questions.

   a. What coins would you use to buy the battery if you paid with 17 coins?

   b. What are the fewest coins you could have used to buy the battery?

3. Refer to problem 4 to answer these questions.

   a. If you were paid $10.00 each time, would you have been better off? Explain.

   b. Suppose it had snowed 20 times. Would you have still been better off being paid $10.00 each time? Explain.

   c. What suggestions do you have for future agreements on shoveling snow?

4. Refer to problem 5 to answer this question. How many of each type ticket could you buy with $25.00 if you bought at least one of each type ticket?

5. *My Journal:* Which problem did you enjoy the most? Why? What strategies did you use to solve it?

BUILDING OPERATIONS SENSE WITH MONEY

It's a 10!

Did you ever wonder how people discovered that you can work with decimals in the same way that you can with whole numbers?

Understanding of the concepts of decimals was evident in works from China and the Middle East long before the 16th century. But in the 16th century the Flemish mathematician, Simon Stevin, published a book that explained the use of decimals in great detail. He thought that adding, subtracting, multiplying, or dividing with fractions was very difficult and that everyone should use decimals. The chart shows how he wrote decimals.

Decimal	Stevin's method
	⓪ ① ② ③
5.426	5 4 2 6

The 0 stands for the 0 power of 10, or 1.

The 1 stands for the $^{-}1$ power of 10, that is 0.1 or $\frac{1}{10}$.

The 2 stands for the $^{-}2$ power of 10, that is 0.01 or $\frac{1}{100}$.

The 3 stands for the $^{-}3$ power of 10, that is 0.001 or $\frac{1}{1000}$.

Stevin also believed everyone should use a base 10 system of weights and measures. And now almost every nation except the United States officially uses the metric system.

· ·

❶ Write three decimals the way you usually do. Then write them as Simon Stevin would have.

❷ Do you think it is easier to work with fractions or decimals? Explain.

❸ What examples of the metric system can you find used in your home or neighborhood?

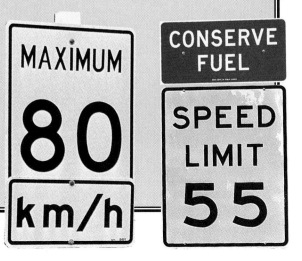

Estimate and Solve

▶ For each problem, estimate the solution. Then find the actual solution using any method you can.

NEW LONG-LIFE
BATTERY
FOR LAPTOPS

We guarantee
1.5 times the
running time!
Try us and see!
Call **555-LONG**

1 A battery for a lap-top computer is advertised as a long-life battery. If your typical battery life is about 90 minutes, about how long might you expect this new battery to last?

2 An estimated 65.9 billion cans and bottles of soft drinks were sold in the United States in 1990. The graph shows what part of this number were sold in each type of container. About how many of each type of container were sold?

PACKAGING OF SOFT
DRINKS FOR 1992

0.751
plastic bottles

0.108

0.141

12-oz cans

glass bottles

3 About how many times greater is the *average-to-date* rainfall than the rainfall for *last-year-to-date*? About how many times greater is the *average-to-date* rainfall than the rainfall *to-date*?

WEATHER / WEEK OF JUNE 14-20

Temperatures

	Mon	Tue	Wed	Thur	Fri	Sat	Sun
highs	77	81	74	74	69	65	72
lows	53	49	48	46	52	44	45

Rainfall

to date	11.40"
last year to date	6.88"
average to date	15.62"

last
quarter
June 26

ESTIMATING
WITH
DECIMALS

4 The chart shows the winning speeds in miles per hour for the champions at the Indianapolis 500 automobile race for every 5 years from 1913 through 1993. Choose any two years that are at least 20 years apart. Tell how many times faster the one speed is than the other.

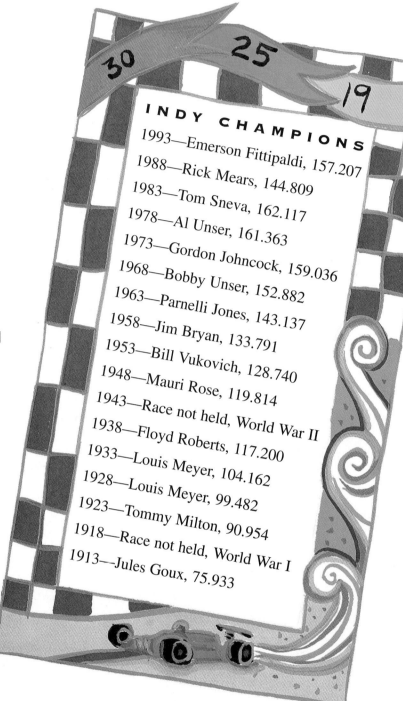

INDY CHAMPIONS
1993—Emerson Fittipaldi, 157.207
1988—Rick Mears, 144.809
1983—Tom Sneva, 162.117
1978—Al Unser, 161.363
1973—Gordon Johncock, 159.036
1968—Bobby Unser, 152.882
1963—Parnelli Jones, 143.137
1958—Jim Bryan, 133.791
1953—Bill Vukovich, 128.740
1948—Mauri Rose, 119.814
1943—Race not held, World War II
1938—Floyd Roberts, 117.200
1933—Louis Meyer, 104.162
1928—Louis Meyer, 99.482
1923—Tommy Milton, 90.954
1918—Race not held, World War I
1913—Jules Goux, 75.933

ON YOUR OWN

▶ Estimate. Then find the exact solution to each problem.

1. Trish swims 1.5 miles a day, 5 days a week. How far does she swim in a week?

2. Laryssa phoned home after a swim meet. She talked for 3.5 minutes at a time when the rate was $.40 per minute. How much did the call cost?

3. Try to cover a row, column, or diagonal.

Follow these steps:

- Choose two factors. Use estimation to help you make your choice.

- Find the product using any method. If that product is in a square, cover it with a counter or penny.

- Continue choosing pairs of factors until you have covered four squares in a row.

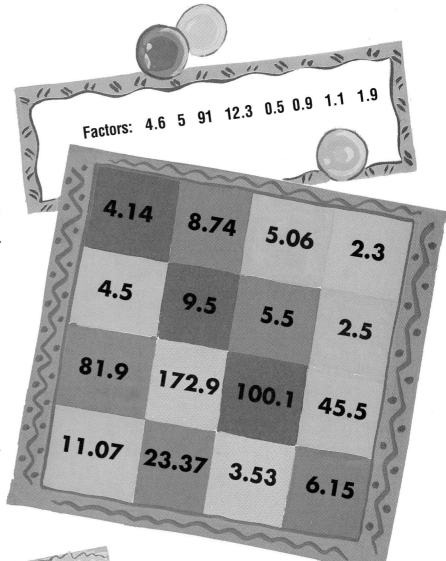

Factors: 4.6 5 91 12.3 0.5 0.9 1.1 1.9

4.14	8.74	5.06	2.3
4.5	9.5	5.5	2.5
81.9	172.9	100.1	45.5
11.07	23.37	3.53	6.15

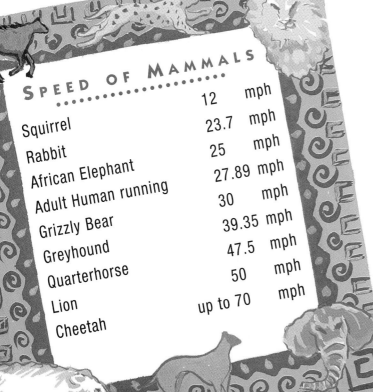

SPEED OF MAMMALS

Squirrel	12 mph
Rabbit	23.7 mph
African Elephant	25 mph
Adult Human running	27.89 mph
Grizzly Bear	30 mph
Greyhound	39.35 mph
Quarterhorse	47.5 mph
Lion	50 mph
Cheetah	up to 70 mph

4. This chart shows the speeds at which mammals can move. Choose any two mammals and tell how many times faster the one speed is than the other.

5. *My Journal:* What have you learned about multiplying decimals?

ESTIMATING
WITH
DECIMALS

87

The Missing Factor Game

Group

4 players

Materials

Each group needs:

A list of factors and product ranges

Round	Factor	Product Range
1	15.4	between 150 and 200
2	18.2	between 60 and 90
3	23.2	between 200 and 250
4	62.7	between 20 and 40
5	89.3	between 50 and 70
6	32.5	between 250 and 300

A score sheet

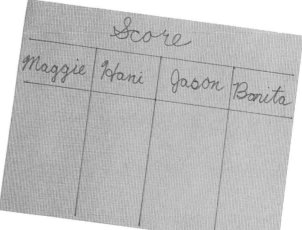

Each player needs:

A calculator

Game Rules

1 Look at the factor for Round 1 and use mental math or estimation to select a number that can be multiplied with that factor to get a product within the range shown. Enter your number into a calculator.

2 Multiply the number you selected by the given factor. If you get a product within the given range, you score 1 point.

3 Continue to play for the remaining five rounds. Whoever has the most points at the end of 6 rounds is the group's winner. There could be a tie.

The Effect of a Surface on Ball Bounce Height

When you drop a ball, it rises to a certain height on the first bounce. What factors might cause this "bounce height" to change?

Conduct an experiment
to find the effect of a surface
on the bounce height of a falling ball.
Follow these steps:

1. Drop a ball ten times from the same height
   onto the same surface.

2. Use a meter stick to measure the height of the ball's
   bounce each time it bounced back.

3. Record each height. Use this data to find the average bounce height.

4. Repeat Steps 1–3 dropping the same ball from the
   same height onto a different type of surface.

Describe your group experiment and data.
Make a class display of data and
analyze it. Write a clear description
of your work and conclusions
explaining how you
used decimals.

Check YOURSELF

Great job! Your report includes a description of the
work your group did, the data your group collected,
an analysis of the data the class collected, and a
conclusion based on the data. Your report explains
your work, your conclusions, and how decimals were
used in the experiments.

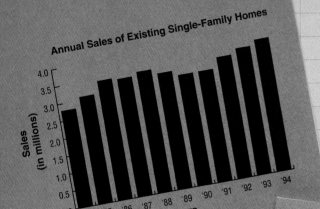

Annual Sales of Existing Single-Family Homes

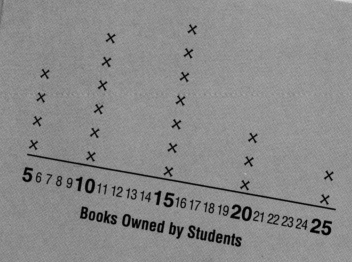

Books Owned by Students

Prices of Video Games

2	9.99
3	5, 6.99, 9.90, 9.90, 9.99, 9.99
4	2.49, 2.49, 2.49, 2.49, 2.49, 4.90, 4.99, 4.99, 4.99, 4.99, 6.90, 8.90, 9.90, 9.90, 9.97, 9.97, 9.99
5	4, 4.99, 6.99

NFL Teams That Have Gone The Longest Without Winning The Division Championships

New York Jets	23
Kansas City	21
Green Bay	20
Phoenix	17
Atlanta	12

*W*hat patterns can we see in data?

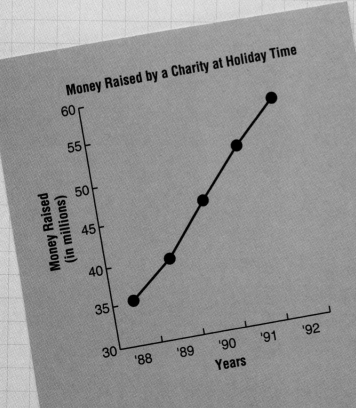

Money Raised by a Charity at Holiday Time

11	9, 9, 9
12	5, 5, 5
13	0, 5, 5, 5, 5
14	0, 5, 5, 5, 5
15	5
16	0
17	1, 1, 1, 1, 1
18	9, 9

Weight of High School Wrestlers

Little Drops of Water

How many drops of water can fit on the surface of a penny before the water overflows?

▶ You need a penny, a cup of water, an eyedropper, and some paper towels.

1. Decide how many samples you need to have enough information to make conclusions.

2. Record your data for each sample.

3. Make a line plot of the data collected by your group.

4. Write about what you observe in the data and any conclusions you can make.

ON YOUR OWN

In this American Indian game, Three Throw Ball, a person has three turns to throw a ball. First a ball is thrown just with the right arm, then with the left, and finally with both arms.

The trick: the thrower has to lie on his or her back to throw the ball.

GENERALIZING
AND
ANALYZING
DATA

95

Three Throw Ball
Distance Thrown (in meters)

Thrower	Right Arm	Left Arm	Both Arms
Anita	3.6	2.9	2.6
Graciela	4.3	3.6	3.0
Richard	2.9	4.7	3.2
Natasha	3.7	3.7	3.5
Cheryl	2.6	2.4	3.2
Seija	4.7	4.5	4.1
Eli	3.2	3.9	3.5
Josh	5.1	3.8	3.5
Claudette	3.3	3.3	3.3

1. How many people are playing Three Throw Ball?

2. Write as many statements as you can that describe the results of the Three Throw Ball game. Use the ideas you learned in this activity.

3. Is there anything surprising about the distances for throws using both arms?

4. *My Journal:* Why do you think analyzing data helps you to discover things that were not obvious at first?

Beat the Clock

Fifteen students were asked how many minutes it takes them to get to school. The results of the survey are shown here.

22, 25, 12, 5, 15, 26, 38, 25,

20, 10, 30, 35, 18, 9, 20

This data can be arranged in a stem-and-leaf plot.

Stem	Leaves
0	5, 9
1	0, 2, 5, 8
2	0, 0, 2, 5, 5, 6
3	0, 5, 8

Why do you think this is called a stem-and-leaf plot?

▶ Try this experiment. How long is one minute?

1 Close your eyes.

2 Your partner records the start time and says "go."

3 You say "stop" when you think exactly 1 minute has passed.

4 Your partner records the actual number of seconds that passed from the "go" to the "stop."

5 Repeat steps 1–4. Record the results separately from the first try.

6 Use the data from the whole class. Make a stem-and-leaf plot for each try.

7 Then make a bar graph for the first try. What information do you get from the stem-and-leaf plot that you do not get from the bar graph?

ESTIMATING
TIME

**ON
YOUR
OWN**

1. Look at the prices
for CDs for 1993
and 1994:

**Cost of the
Top 25 CDs in 1994**

$12.25; $13.50; $18.35;

$11.49; $16.75; $12.75;

$15.50; $11.69; $10.25;

$15.25; $14.50; $17.99;

$11.79; $13.35; $11.35;

$14.25; $11.79; $12.99;

$10.49; $16.50; $11.49;

$12.75; $14.75; $11.99;

$10.99

**Cost of the
Top 25 CDs in 1993**

$12.55; $18.25; $14.25;

$15.39; $17.35; $17.29;

$13.49; $13.69; $14.25;

$15.50; $13.69; $14.25;

$16.99; $14.25; $13.99

$16.65; $12.69; $12.89

$13.99; $15.38; $17.69;

$13.45; $15.75; $12.69

$13.69

1993 CD Prices

$18	.25
$17	.29, .35, .69
$16	.65, .99
$15	
$14	
$13	
$12	

1994 CD Prices

$18	
$17	
$16	
$15	
$14	
$13	
$12	
$11	
$10	

a. Copy and complete these
stem-and-leaf plots. Use
the prices above.

b. Use your stem-and-leaf plots to write all the
comparison statements you can. Explain any
differences you see.

2. Look at the results for each race.

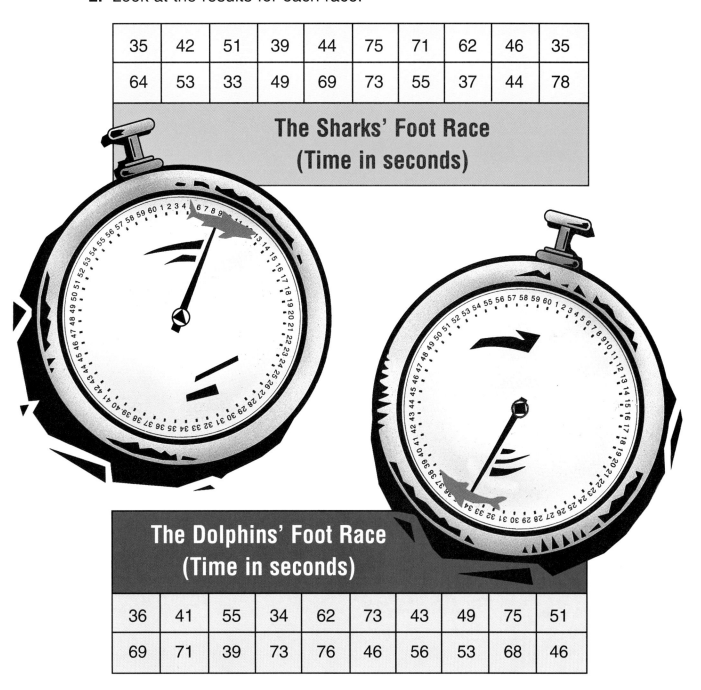

| 35 | 42 | 51 | 39 | 44 | 75 | 71 | 62 | 46 | 35 |
| 64 | 53 | 33 | 49 | 69 | 73 | 55 | 37 | 44 | 78 |

The Sharks' Foot Race
(Time in seconds)

The Dolphins' Foot Race
(Time in seconds)

| 36 | 41 | 55 | 34 | 62 | 73 | 43 | 49 | 75 | 51 |
| 69 | 71 | 39 | 73 | 76 | 46 | 56 | 53 | 68 | 46 |

a. Make a stem-and-leaf plot for each data table.

b. Write as many comparisons as you can about the foot races.

3. *My Journal:* Why might a stem-and-leaf plot be better than a bar graph for comparing data?

Some Like it Hot, Some Like it Cold

Some cities in North America and their average temperatures

Juneau 40°f

51°f. Vancouver

Kansas City 54°f

Chicago 49°f

Toronto 46°f

40°f. Quebec City

52°f. Boston

San Francisco 57°f

Denver 50°f

Los Angeles 63°f

Detroit 49°f

58°f Washington, D.C.

55°f. New York City

Phoenix 71°f

Dallas · Ft. Worth 66°f

61°f. Atlanta

New Orleans 68°f

76°f. Miami

Honolulu 77°f

Mexico City 61°f

80°f

San Juan

80°f Acapulco

SHOWING TEMPERATURE

	City	High Temperature	Low Temperature
1	Juneau, AK	64	16
2	Phoenix, AZ	105	39
3	Los Angeles, CA	77	47
4	San Juan, PR	88	70
5	Denver, CO	88	16
6	Washington, DC	88	28
7	Miami, FL	89	59
8	Atlanta, GA	88	65
9	San Francisco, CA	73	42
10	Honolulu, HI	88	65
11	Chicago, IL	83	14
12	New Orleans, LA	91	43
13	Boston, MA	82	23
14	Detroit, MI	83	16
15	Kansas City, MO	89	17
16	New York, NY	85	26
17	Philadelphia, PA	86	24
18	Dallas-Ft. Worth, TX	98	34
19	Quebec City, Quebec	48	31
20	Toronto, Ontario	54	37
21	Vancouver, British Columbia	58	43
22	Acapulco, Guerrero	87	73
23	Mexico City, Federal District	72	50

ON YOUR OWN

Volcano Name	Feet Above Sea Level	Last Major Eruption
Cinder Cone	6,907	1851
Lassen Peak	10,453	1914–1921
Mt. Shasta	14,161	1855
Mt. Hood	11,245	1801
Mt. Baker	10,778	1870
Mt. Rainier	14,410	1882
Mt. St. Helens	8,364	1984
Haleakala	10,025	1790
Hualalai	8,251	1801
Kilauea	4,090	1984
Mauna Loa	13,680	1984
Kiska	4,025	1969
Little Sitkin	3,945	1828
Cerberus	2,560	1873
Gareloi	5,370	1930
Tanaga	5,925	1914
Kanaga	4,450	1933
Great Sitkin	5,775	1945
Keniuji	885	1828

1. The data to the right is displayed in a table. Choose another way to display the data. Then write five questions about your display. Exchange your display and questions with a classmate, then answer each other's questions.

2. *My Journal:* Explain why you think stem-and-leaf plots are valuable.

Long Ago Lengths

▶ These charts show the approximate lengths of 65 different dinosaurs. Use this information to make a stem-and-leaf plot and a line plot.

Compsognathus	3 feet
Ornitholestes	6 feet
Coelophysis	10 feet
Oviraptor	5 feet
Struthiomimus	12 feet
Dromiceiomimus	12 feet
Segisaurus	3 feet
Avimimus	5 feet
Segnosaur	15 feet
Stenonychosaurus	6 feet
Saurornithoides	6 feet
Ceratosaurus	20 feet
Dilophosaurus	20 feet

Allosaurus	39 feet
Tyrannosaurus	46 feet
Daspletosaurus	29 feet
Albertosaurus	29 feet
Anchisaurus	8 feet
Plateosaurus	24 feet
Apatosaurus	69 feet
Diplodocus	88 feet
Camarasaurus	59 feet
Brachiosaurus	74 feet
Opisthocoelicaudia	39 feet
Saltasaurus	39 feet
Vulcanodon	21 feet

Lesothosaurus	3 feet
Heterodontosaurus	4 feet
Scutellosaurus	4 feet
Hypsilophodon	6 feet
Dryosaurus	12 feet
Tenontosaurus	18 feet
Camptosaurus	20 feet
Ouranosaurus	23 feet
Muttaburrasaurus	23 feet
Iguanodon	33 feet
Bactrosaurus	15 feet
Kritosaurus	30 feet
Anatosaurus	35 feet

Edmontosaurus	35 feet
Protoceratops	6 feet
Psittacosaurus	6 feet
Tsintaosaurus	23 feet
Saurolophus	35 feet
Corythosaurus	33 feet
Parasaurolophus	33 feet
Styracosaurus	18 feet
Centrosaurus	20 feet
Triceratops	29 feet
Chasmosaurus	17 feet
Anchiceratops	20 feet
Pentaceratops	23 feet

Torosaurus	25 feet
Stegoceras	6 feet
Homalocephale	10 feet
Pachycephalosaurus	26 feet
Stegosaurus	22 feet
Tuojiangosaurus	20 feet
Kentrosaurus	8 feet
Scelidosaurus	13 feet
Hylaeosaurus	13 feet
Polacanthus	13 feet
Nodosaurus	18 feet
Pinacosaurus	16 feet
Euoplocephalus	20 feet

Deer Friends

The mean and median weights for different types of deer are given on these pages.

Lapland Reindeer

3 feet 6 inches tall
mean = 300 pounds
median = 305 pounds

Alaskan Moose

7 feet 6 inches high at the shoulder
mean = 1,650 pounds
median = 1,625 pounds

Japanese Sika

30 inches tall
mean = 80 pounds
median = 75 pounds

American Elk

5 feet high at the shoulder
mean = 850 pounds
median = 875 pounds

Caribou

4 feet tall
mean = 300 pounds
median = 300 pounds

Indian Barasingha

5 feet high at the shoulder
mean = 450 pounds
median = 440 pounds

Indian Sambar

over 5 feet tall
mean = 700 pounds
median = 725 pounds

Chilean Rabbit Deer

1 foot tall
mean = 20 pounds
median = 22 pounds

ON YOUR OWN

1. Create a set of six data points where the median is greater than the mean.

2. Tell whether each is true or false:

   a. The mean is always one of the numbers in a list of numbers.

   b. Mean and average are the same.

   c. The mean and the median are always the same.

   d. If there is one middle number in a list, it is the median.

   e. The mode only appears once in a list of numbers.

3. Find the mean height of the people in your household.

4. Use mental math to estimate the mean for the following numbers: 95, 187, 220, 230, 299, 302, 489, 575.

5. *My Journal:* What questions do you still have about the mean, median, and mode?

Information From Cords to CARDS

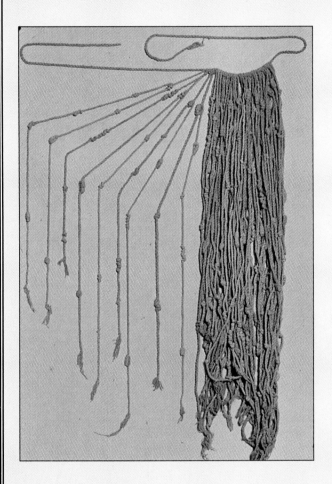

Have you ever wondered how people took a census before the powerful computers of today?

Years ago the Inca in Peru used knotted ropes called quipu. The quipu used a decimal system. A knot in a row farthest from the main rope indicated 1, the next knot closer in represented 10 and so on. To show the population on a quipu different colors were used for men, women and children.

In the 1890 census in the United States information was collected on key punch cards for the first data processing machines. By 1950, the computer was used for the United States census.

1 What do you think the benefits of using key punch cards were?

2 Why do you think computers are now used to store data for the census? What are the advantages?

3 Invent your own method of recording and storing data on a cord or a card.

Oh, Say Can You See

▶ Materials:

Cardboard tube from
a roll of paper towels
Meter stick
Tape

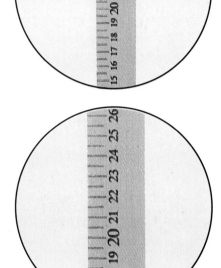

1 Tape the meter stick to the wall, with the zero line about 1 meter from the floor.

2 Measure a length of 3 meters from the wall and use tape to mark this spot on the floor.

3 Stand so that the toes of your shoes are on the tape mark on the floor.

4 Look through the tube and record the length of the meter stick you can see. You will need to subtract the smaller number from the greater number.

5 Repeat this experiment several times, moving the tape mark on the floor to 2.5 meters, 2.0 meters, and so on. Record the distances and the lengths you see.

► Use the data below to answer the questions. Different tubes were used to generate the data below. Follow the directions and answer the questions to find out which tube was used for each set of data.

1. Construct a line graph for each set of data.

2. What length of the meter stick might you see with the tube that generated the Set 1 data placed at 1.75 meters from the wall? Explain.

Distance from wall (in meters)	SET 1 Length observed (cm)	SET 2 Length observed (cm)	SET 3 Length observed (cm)
0.5	15	10	6
1.0	28	19	12
1.5	45	29	19
2.0	62	41	25
2.5	78	53	31
3.0	94	63	37

3. What do you think is the shortest distance from the wall where you can stand and see the entire meter stick? Which tube will you use to find the shortest distance? Explain.

4. Using the tube that generated the Set 3 data, about how much of the meter stick would you see at a distance of 4 meters?

5. Match Tubes A, B, and C with the appropriate data sets. Explain your reasoning.

6. *My Journal:* What can you learn from line graphs?

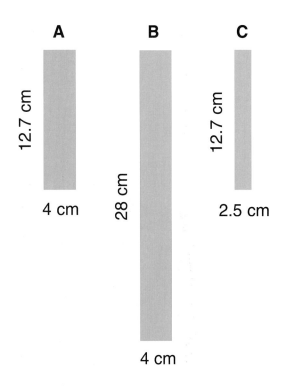

The Time in a Week

How do you spend the time in a week? Estimate the times for different activities. Then keep track to check your estimates.

Choose one activity. Then write a questionnaire to collect your data. Display the survey results in a graph and find ways to analyze them.

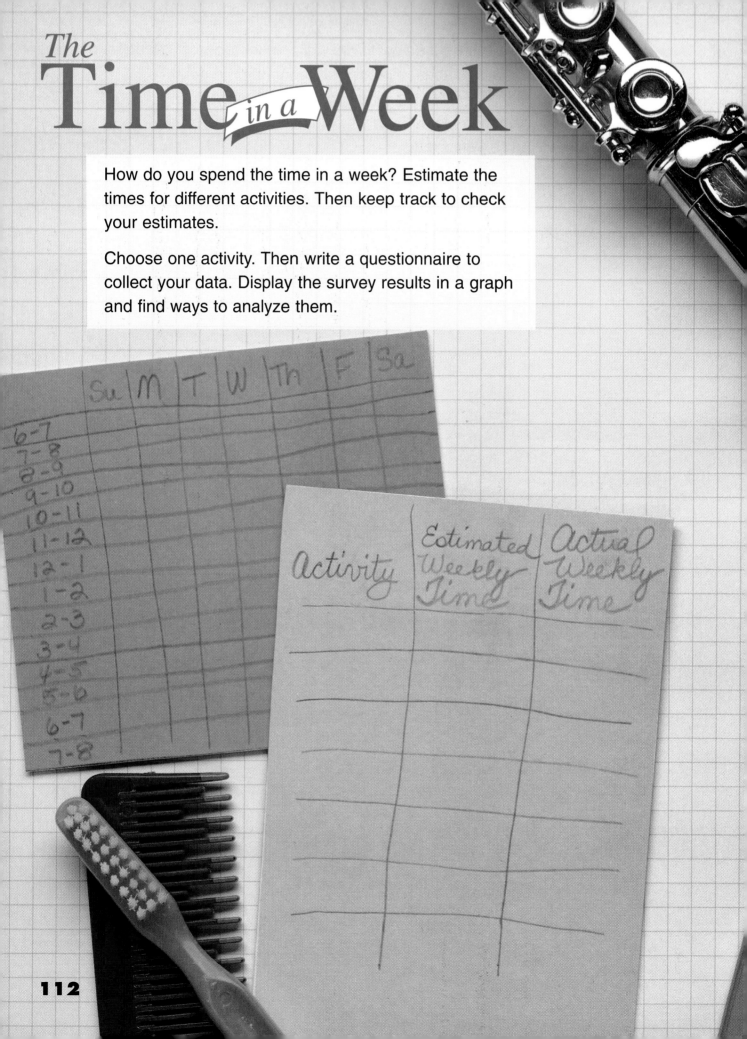

	Su	M	T	W	Th	F	Sa
6-7							
7-8							
8-9							
9-10							
10-11							
11-12							
12-1							
1-2							
2-3							
3-4							
4-5							
5-6							
6-7							
7-8							

Activity	Estimated Weekly Time	Actual Weekly Time

STUDENT RESOURCE BOOK

CheckYOURSELF

Great job! You collected the data thoroughly and accurately. The graph you chose to explain your data gave a good picture. You used ideas such as mean, median, and mode to help explain the data. You wrote how these various numbers, together with the graph, helped you analyze the data.

What is a good sample?

Four Out of Five Students Love This Page

▶ Each of the following statements was made using data from a sample. As you read these, think about who the sample might have been and whether those surveyed are representative of the population.

ON YOUR OWN

▶ Try the hand clasp experiment or another like it with people at home or friends. Tally the results in a table like this one:

Hand Clasping	
Left Thumb	
Right Thumb	

1. How many people are in the sample?

2. Describe the results of your sample.

3. For what population are your results a sampling?

4. How do the results of your sample at home compare to the class data?

5. *My Journal:* Do you think statements made from a sample are always accurate for a population? Explain.

Predicting How Many

▶ Choose two of the questions below.

For each, choose and describe a sample to survey and record the results. Use your results to make a prediction for the whole class. Then compile class results using a line plot to test your predictions.

How did your predictions compare with the actual results for the population?

1. What is your favorite food for lunch?

2. What is your favorite flavor of ice cream?

3. How many hours of TV do you watch in a typical day?

4. Do you prefer Westerns, Cartoons or News programs?

Making Predictions

```
        5 3 # # $ 3 0 5
      ) ) 6 * ; 4 8 2 6 ) 4 #
    . ) 4 # ; 8 0 6 * ; 4 8 $ 8
    @ 6 0 ) ) 8 5 ; & # ( ; : # *
  8 $ 8 3 ( 8 8 ) 5 * $ ; 4 6 ( ; 8
  8 * 9 6 * ? ; 8 ) * # ( ; 4 8 5 )
; 5 * $ 2 : * # ( ; 4 9 5 6 * 2 ( 5 *
 − 4 ) 8 @ 8 * ; 4 0 6 9 2 8 5 ) ; )
  6 $ 8 ) 4 # # ; & ( # 9 ; 4 8 0 8
  & ; 8 : 8 # & ; 4 8 $ 8 5 ; 4 ) 4
    8 5 $ 5 2 8 8 0 6 * 8 & ( # 9 ;
      4 8 ; ( 8 8 ; 4 ( # ? 3 4 ;
      4 8 ) 4 # ; & 6 & ; : & 8
          8 ; # ? ;
```

you would find in an article using 10,000 words. How many would be in a story using 50,000 words? Would you want to check your predictions?

Now think about other languages. What do you think would be the most common letters in Spanish? Are there languages whose letters or symbols you don't know? If you or any of your classmates know a language other than English, discuss how to find the most-used letters or symbols.

Have you ever wondered which five letters are used most often in the English language?

Make a guess and write the letters down.

How could you check your guess? What size sample should you check? How should you begin? If you work with a group you can divide the work. After you have completed your sample, predict how many of each letter

1 Why would code makers and code breakers be interested in what letters appear most often?

2 The code above was used by Edgar Allan Poe in "The Gold Bug." Can you use what you learned about letters in English to break it?

3 The Navajo language as spoken by Navajo "Code Talkers" was important to the United States military in World War II. Find out why.

The SAMPLE Game

Play several rounds of this guessing game with a partner.

Materials

Paper bag
10 counters of each of three colors

Rules

1. Player 1 places 10 counters, at least one of each color, in the bag without Player 2 seeing.

2. Player 2 draws one counter and does not put it back in the bag. Player 1 tallies the draw in a chart.

3. Player 2 continues to draw one counter at a time without replacing it and Player 1 records each draw in the tally chart.

4. Play continues like this until Player 2 is ready to predict how many counters of each color were placed in the bag.

5. Player 1 empties the bag, finds the totals, and compares them with Player 2's prediction.

To score a round:

Player 2 gets:
1 point for each correct prediction for a color and a bonus of 3 points if all three colors are correct.

1 point for each counter left in the bag when a correct prediction was made for that color.

2 points for each remaining counter when correct predictions were made for all three colors.

Player 1 and Player 2 swap roles and repeat the activity. After 3 rounds the player with the higher score wins.

ON YOUR OWN

▶ Imagine that you are playing a round of The Sample Game.

1. Draw a bag with 10 counters in it that might have been used to get the tallies shown below. Explain your decision.

2. Draw two different pairs of bags with 20 counters in them that might have been used to get the tallies shown. Explain your decisions.

3. If you had to choose between watching football or tennis, which would you watch?

   Franco asked 40 of his friends, all boys, this question. Based on their answers, he concluded that football would be the choice for all 205 students in the school.

   But Maria asked the first 20 students who passed her in the hall the same question. From this sample, she concluded that tennis is the sport that students prefer.

   Explain in writing which, if either, conclusion you think is best and why you think so.

4. *My Journal:* What have you learned about how a sample may or may not be a good predictor of a population?

Common Letters

▶ Which letter is used the most frequently in a newspaper? Here's one way to find out.

1. Select a typical page from a newspaper.

2. Predict which letter is the most common on the newpaper page. Record your prediction.

3. Drop a paper clip onto the newspaper. The letter closest to the end of the paper clip is the one you should record and count.

4. Take 25 samples by dropping the paper clip 25 times.

5. Record your data in a chart that displays the sample total, each letter that occurred, and how often it occurred.

6. What is the most common letter? Are you sure?

7. Take 25 more samples by dropping the paper clip 25 more times, for a total of 50 samples. Continue to record in your chart.

8. What is the most common letter? Are you sure? Did the extra 25 samples make a difference?

9. Take 25 more samples, and then 25 more.

10. Continue to record your data in the chart.

11. Does each sample make you more sure of your choice? Explain your reasoning.

ON YOUR OWN

1. Do all materials written in English have the same most common letters? What do you think? Why do you think so? Select another kind of material and sample the letters using the procedure you used in studying the newspaper. Present your results and your explanation.

2. Do all languages that use the same alphabet have the same most common letters? Take a sample of some languages that you find. Bring materials from home or elsewhere that you can test.

gue sintiendo absolutamente adscrita a la alta
azar podrá llevar de aquí para allá en el esp
sico y en el social. No importa: ella seguirá es
junto a quien ama. Este es el síntoma supre
el verdadero amor, estar al lado de lo amado
contacto y proximidad más profundos que
paciales. Es un estar vitalmente en el otro. La
bra más exacta, pero demasiado técnica, es e
estar con el amado, fiel al destino de este, se
e sea". El que ama no solo queda adscrito al
ara siempre, sino que asume su vida con una
encia y esperanza infinitas como las del coro
de esperar al otro se trata. No en vano está

tucja przerwy utworow były popularne
jest menuety Beethovena, Mar z
vania militarny i impromptu Schubrta
mów oraz fragmenty z jego symf ni
h w transkrypcje pieśn
13. Mendelssohna i romantyczne
i Marzenie Schumanna.
wego Muzyka zamilkła (r.estety, nie
trum wszyscy goście podczas
tego inauguracyjnych przemówień i
dla pierwszych rozmów
T&T wideotelefonicznych z Warszawą.
a, że Dr Marcin Sar ciekawie i z pasją
ętnie mówił o historycznych i
ne i technicznych tajemnicach
ka, a wielkiej reprodukcji
iego sztychów z XV-XVI w

ranowskiego w Łowi
ieleński był na
muzykiem, ale również
ośrodkach muzycznych
Otóż, patrząc na
panoramę starego V
(Vratislavia — złaty
forma czeska, starop
Wrocisław) kojarzym
faktem, że częsc
muzycznej na głosy
polscy muzykolodzy w
bibliotece miejskie
Wrocławiu (część org
Krakowie). Po wojnie
Zieleńskiego odżyła r
odnowionej katedrze i k

nal Plus, Philippe Koechlin interroge dans
la rue des inconnus, qui s'extasient avec
un bel aplomb : « Ah ! Bechet ! Il est for-
midable, un grand trompettiste ! » Cette
naïve popularité, cette renommée pleine
d'à peu près, sont cause sans doute d'une
bonne part de la réputation ambigüe de
Bechet. A titre posthume, il ne lui sera pas
pardonné d'avoir eu ses 45-tours dans
tous les juke-boxes de France. Les pu-
ristes de l'avant garde feront de lui un re-
poussoir. Il sera prétendu de bon goût

3. *My Journal:* Do you think sampling is a useful technique? When do you think it might be useful? Explain.

AMAZING FACTS

The Hawaiian alphabet has only 12 letters:

H, K, L, M, N, P, W, A, E, I, O, *and* U.

How Do We Compare?

1. How many television sets do you have in your home? (National average is 1.9)

2. How many hours of TV do you watch each week? (National average for all ages and sexes is about 20 hours.)

3. Do you read a newspaper every day? (71% or about seven tenths of Americans do.)

4. Do you read a book or part of one for pleasure each day? (One third of Americans say they do.)

5. Would you stop watching television altogether for $1 million? (One fourth of people asked said they would stop.)

6. How many radios do you have in your home? Include portable types. (In 1988 there were an average 5.6 radios in each home.)

7. How many times do you eat away from home each week? (Half of all people in the United States eat out once a day—or seven times a week.)

8. How many magazines do you read in a day? (One third of the people in the United States claim to read a magazine a day.)

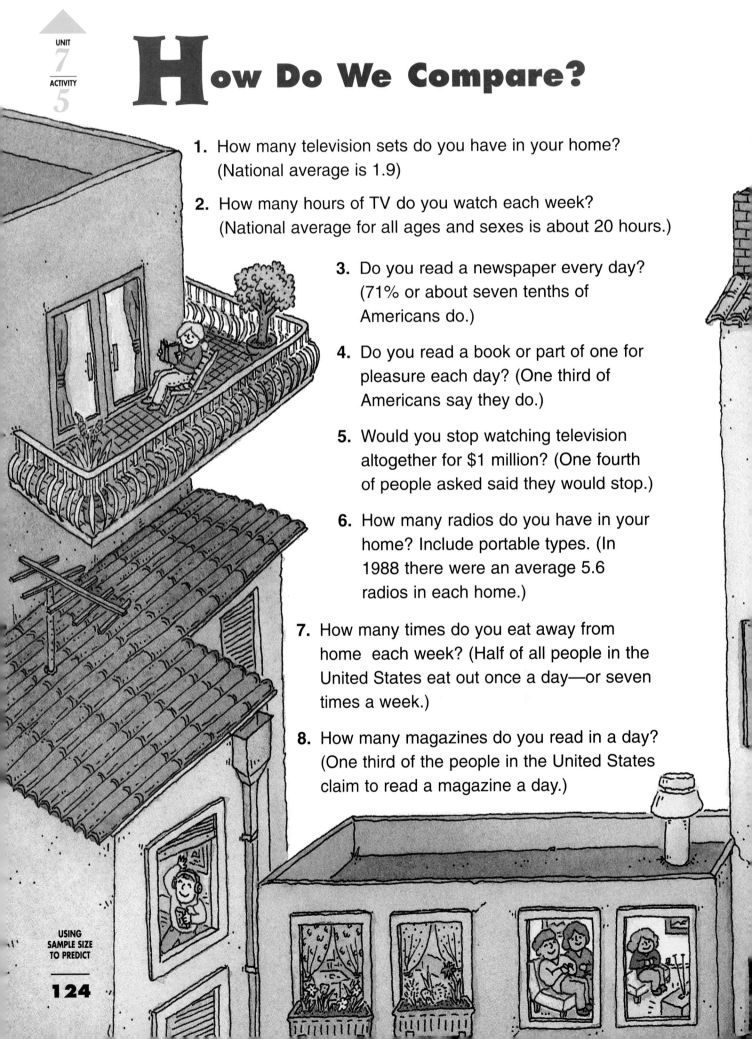

ON YOUR OWN

▶ Interview one or two adults at home. Ask them the three questions in your class survey about television and the three about reading habits.

1. How do their answers compare with the answers found for your class?

2. How do their answers compare with the national data?

3. *My Journal:* Do you think a sample as small as the population of your class or the parents of your classmates is useful as a predictor of a population as large as the United States? Explain why or why not.

Taking a School Opinion Survey

Do you think you know what the other students in your school think or believe about various questions? One way to find out is to select a good sample and take an opinion survey.

How long do you think the school day should be?

Do we need more crossing guards near the school?

Should students in our school be fined for littering?

Survey-Taking Guide

1. What is the population we want to use? What size sample do we need to take?

2. What do we want to learn about the population?

3. What does it mean for a sample to be representative of a population? What can we do to try to make our sample representative?

4. How can we state our question so that it is easy to understand, and so that we can interpret the answers more easily?

SURVEY TALLY

Question:

Students who answered YES:

Students who answered NO:

TOTAL YES:
TOTAL NO:

*C*heck **Y**OURSELF

Great job! Your survey plans, data collection, and report were complete and accurate. You wrote to explain how you chose your sample and why it represents the entire school's population.

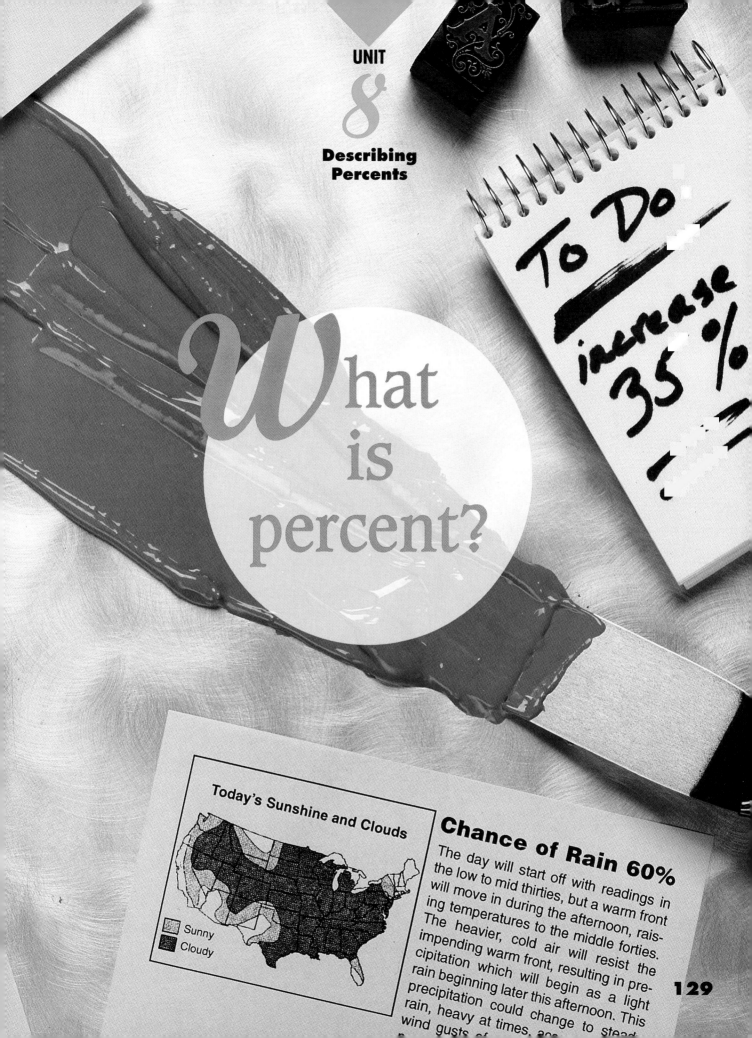

*W*hat is percent?

TO DO

increase
35%

Today's Sunshine and Clouds

Sunny
Cloudy

Chance of Rain 60%

The day will start off with readings in the low to mid thirties, but a warm front will move in during the afternoon, raising temperatures to the middle forties. The heavier, cold air will resist the impending warm front, resulting in precipitation which will begin as a light rain beginning later this afternoon. This precipitation could change to steady rain, heavy at times, acc... wind gusts of...

Percents All Around

major banks became a regular feature in most newspapers as the prime zig-zagged from a record high of 20% in April down to 10¾% in July and back up to a new all-time high of 21½% in December... the massive swing... in the...

ization in a... 15%; ● Mai...

Gallon Sales	Unit Case Sales
1%	3%
(19)%	(18)%
27%	30%
16%	

Average Annual Yield
Outperformed peer groups

22.2%
18.1%
17.5%
17.3%

Percent

S&P 400
S&P 500
Dow Jones Industrial Average

Chile 4%
Colombia 6%
Argentina 10%

Other
15%

Mexico
43%

Brazil
22%

MORTGAGE
6 1/4% 6. 65% APR

Stocks and Bonds
Up To 76%
If you...

Save

% Change
15.2
10.2
17.4
14.0
31.0
5.6
4.9
14.1

...us great opportunities and challenges is to become a global company, and we are well along on that road. Five years ago, 13% of our sales were international. Since then, such sales have increased 174%, which is an even more rapid pace of expansion than our

20% DISCOUNT
EVERY ITEM ~ EVERY DAY
THOUSANDS IN STOCK
...made • Custom • Recovering
Mountings & Repairs
...rs Experience

"The weather forecast shows 40% chance of rain tonight followed by clearing skies in the morning."

ANGE	% CHG
¼	+ 12.5
¾	+ 12.5
¾	+ 9.8
+ 8.8
+ 8.0
+ 7.7
6.3
5.6
5.6
5.2
5.1
0

...this ambitious political and economic... ...his nation's u... challenges at home. ▶ A landmark U.S.-Soviet... about 90% complete. In an exclusive... Talbott tells the...

Investment
...up 43.7%!*
...s Fund
...nt survey...

AMAZING
FACTS

Less than one-third (about 29%) of the earth's surface is land.

...e workers

...% OF YIE...

100

88—

...Sound area "was a...

ONE WEEK ONLY 20...
Protect the beauty of yo...
exact spe...

ON YOUR OWN

▶ Use these three squares as benchmarks to estimate what percent of each square is shaded in the figures below. Write each estimate using the percent symbol (%).

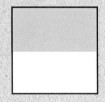  

0% shaded   50% shaded   100% shaded

1.  **2.**  **3.**  **4.**

▶ Draw a square and then shade part of it to show the given percent.

5. about 60%   **6.** about 15%

7. about 90%   **8.** about 35%

9. Talk with family members or neighbors about ways they use percent in their daily lives. Keep a list to share with classmates.

10. *My Journal:* Write what you already know about percent.

Designing Floor Plans

▶ What percent is each room?

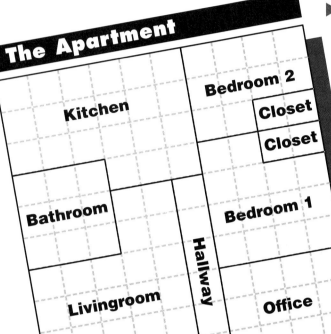

The Apartment

Kitchen

Bedroom 2

Closet

Closet

Bathroom

Bedroom 1

Hallway

Livingroom

Office

▶ Use a 10 × 10 grid to show the floor plan for this office.

The Office Building

Room or Area	Number of Squares	Percent of Floor Space
Waiting Room	12	12%
Copying and Storage	21	21%
Bathroom	6	6%
Office No. 1	30	30%
Office No. 2	20	20%
Hall	11	11%

Tip

When you draw your floor plans, label all the rooms and spaces you have created. Be sure to work in pencil; you may need to make changes in your plans.

▶ Use a 10 × 10 grid to draw a plan for one section of a school building.

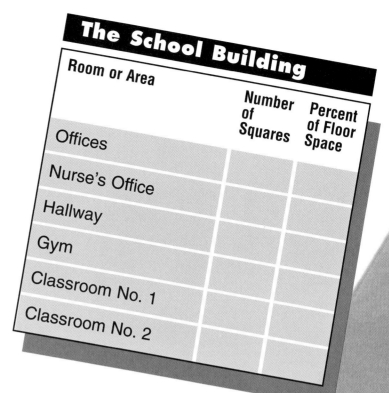

The School Building		
Room or Area	Number of Squares	Percent of Floor Space
Offices		
Nurse's Office		
Hallway		
Gym		
Classroom No. 1		
Classroom No. 2		

ON YOUR OWN

Create a design for a space in your home. You may ask a family member to be your assistant.

1a. Choose a room or area in your home. Recreate it on centimeter grid paper. It will be easier if you use a space that you can show on a 10 × 10 grid.

b. Make a list of the furniture you want to include in your plan.

c. Estimate to determine the percent of the space each piece of furniture should take up. Record the number of squares needed for each.

d. Draw your design. Label all parts.

2. *My Journal:* After you have made a floor plan and labeled the percent for each room what are some ways to check that the percents are correct?

Estimating Floor Space

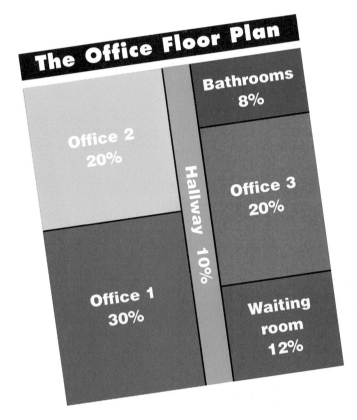

The Office Floor Plan

Bathrooms 8%

Office 2 20%

Hallway 10%

Office 3 20%

Office 1 30%

Waiting room 12%

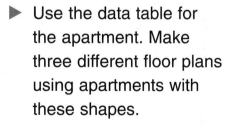

The Apartment

Room or Area	Percent of Floor Space
Living room	35%
Kitchen	15%
Bedroom No. 1	18%
Bedroom No. 2	15%
Bathroom	10%
Closet No. 1	2%
Closet No. 2	5%

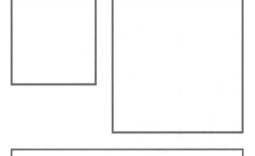

▶ Use the data table for the apartment. Make three different floor plans using apartments with these shapes.

ON YOUR OWN

▶ Copy the figures onto grid paper. Color them as described.

1. Color or shade about 60% of the rectangle.

2. Color or shade the square to show four sections of 25% each.

3. Color or shade the rectangle to show 50%. Then use 3 other colors or shadings and 3 different percents to fill in the rest of the figure. Write the percents next to the colors you use.

▶ Look at the circles. Estimate the percent for each letter. Tell how you decided.

4.  **5.**  **6.**

7. Make a circle graph with 4 sections. Estimate the percent for each section.

▶ Look at these circles. Do the labels seem sensible to you? Explain.

8. **9.** **10.**

11. Make a circle graph that does not make sense. Explain why your graph is not reasonable.

12. *My Journal:* What do you know about percent and the size and shape of the whole unit?

PERCENT OF
THE WHOLE

Percents Line Up

► For each line segment below, draw and label one that is about the same length. Then estimate to label points to show 25%, 50%, and 75% of each.

1 0% ——————— 100%

2 0% ——————————————— 100%

3 0% ——————— 100%

► Copy these line segments. Label them to show 0% and 100%. Then label your estimate for $33\frac{1}{3}\%$ and $66\frac{2}{3}\%$ of each.

4 ————————————

5 ————

► Copy these line segments. Use the information shown to label the 100% point for each. Extend a line segment if necessary.

6 0%   50%

7 0%   75%

8 0% 25%

9 Suppose the people at the right are standing in a line for carnival tickets and the ticket seller estimates that there are enough tickets left for only 75% of them. About how many people will not get tickets?

PERCENT
RELATIVE TO
THE WHOLE

136

ON YOUR OWN

Sense or Nonsense?

▶ Tell whether each statement makes sense or does not make sense. For those that do not, write to explain why.

1. Martita said she is 50% taller than Erin.

2. Pia read 137 pages of a 200-page book. She estimates that she has read about 45% of the book.

3. Ralph spent 100% of his allowance last week. Nico spent about half of his, and said he is sure he spent more than Ralph.

4. The sales tax is less than 10%.

5. Irene told Bob she agreed with his plan 100%, except for his ideas about the estimated budget.

SUBTOTAL	$45.95
TAX	$ 3.22
TOTAL	$49.17

THANK YOU

6. George says that 20% off means that you always save $20.

7. Sue Lee saw that she will save about $10 if she buys a stuffed animal on sale.

STUFFED ANIMAL
REGULARLY $25

10% OFF TODAY

8. *My Journal:* Give a situation where estimating percent is difficult. Tell why it is difficult. Now give one where it is easy to estimate the percent. Tell why.

Healthy BY Percent

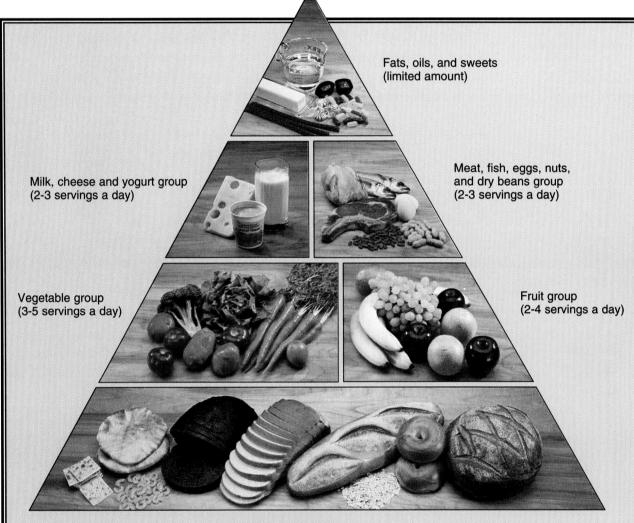

Fats, oils, and sweets
(limited amount)

Milk, cheese and yogurt group
(2-3 servings a day)

Meat, fish, eggs, nuts,
and dry beans group
(2-3 servings a day)

Vegetable group
(3-5 servings a day)

Fruit group
(2-4 servings a day)

Breads, cereals, rice, and pasta group
(6-11 servings a day)

Have you ever wondered if your diet is as healthful as someone else's?

Here's a way to find out. Write down everything you eat for a day. Write what you eat and how much. Look at the nutritional information on boxes, packages, in cook books, or in special books to find out how many calories you ate. Then identify the food group each food belongs in and estimate the percent of calories for each food group. Watch out for fats!

Exchange your data with a partner and compare the healthfulness of your diets. Then select a meal with foods of different origins. Check the foods for nutrients and calories. Discuss and compare your information. How is the food you eat similar to the food you researched? How is it different? In which food is there very little fat? Are any essential nutrients missing? Do you think you would like to try some of the foods you researched? What is important for a healthful diet, no matter which foods you're looking at?

The chance of RAIN or SNOW

How can you use a spinner to model a rain/snow prediction chart?

Group

pair

Materials

1 blank spinner and 1 paperclip (per pair)

The table below shows five cities and the number of days in certain months on which more than 0.01 inch of rain/snow is expected.

Days with More than 0.01 Inch of Rain/Snow						
City	**January**		**June**		**October**	
	No.	**%**	**No.**	**%**	**No.**	**%**
San Francisco, CA	11	36%	1	3%	4	13%
Denver, CO	6	19%	9	30%	5	16%
Buffalo, NY	20	65%	10	33%	12	39%
Cleveland, OH	16	52%	11	37%	11	35%
Seattle, WA	19	61%	9	30%	13	42%

Directions

. . . .

NO RAIN

RAIN

DENVER IN JUNE

1 Work with a partner. Pick one city and one month from the table.

2 Make a spinner that has one section shaded approximately equal to the percent given in the table for the city and month you selected.

3 You will spin your spinner either 30 or 31 times, depending on the number of days in the month you selected. When the spinner lands on the shaded section, you will record a day with rain/snow.

4 Before you begin, predict the number of rainy/snowy days you will get. Write and tell how you made your prediction.

5 Perform the experiment and record your results. How close did your results come to the predicted number?

6 Repeat the experiment. How close were the results to your prediction this time?

7 Compare your results with those of other pairs.

AMAZING
F A C T S

On July 25-26, 1979, at Alvin, Texas 19 inches of rain fell in 24 hours. What is the greatest amount of rain that has fallen in one 24-hour period where you live?

CHANCE
EXPRESSED AS
A PERCENT

ON YOUR OWN

▶ Tell whether each statement makes sense or does not make sense. For those that do not, write to explain why.

1. Look at the table on page 140 for January in San Francisco. It is January 24th and there has been only 1 day of rain. The weather forecaster says, "Looking at our records, it appears that it should rain every day next week."

2. Using the table on page 140, Sharon said that in general you can expect more than three times as much rain in Buffalo, NY, than in Denver, CO during January.

3. There's a 75% chance of rain today. It rained on the way to school. Does this mean it won't rain on the way home from school? Explain.

4. The paper reported a 90% chance of rain. Does this mean it will rain for 90% of the day, or about 22 out of 24 hours? Explain.

5. The morning news said there was a 50% chance of rain, so Rob decided to flip a coin to decide whether or not to take an umbrella.

6. Yesterday there was a 75% chance of rain and it rained for 30 minutes. Today there was also a 75% chance of rain and it rained for 3 hours! Was the prediction incorrect for either day? Explain.

7. Record the chances of precipitation for your town for one week. On how many days did the forecast come true?

8. *My Journal:* Describe what you know about how percents are used in weather forecasting.

Is a fraction less than 1 closest to
0%, 25%, 50%, 75%, or 100%?

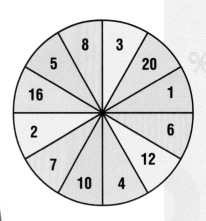

Group

pair

Materials

Paperclip (per pair)

Directions

1 Spin the spinner twice.

2 Use the two numbers to make a fraction less than 1.

3 Estimate whether the fraction you made is closer to 0%, 25%, 50%, 75%, or 100%. Write and tell how you decided.

4 Make a chart to record which percent is the closest.

5 Include at least 10 fractions in your chart.

Fraction	Closest Percent (check one)				
	0%	25%	50%	75%	100%

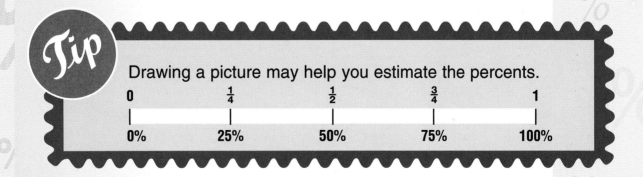

Tip

Drawing a picture may help you estimate the percents.

0	$\frac{1}{4}$	$\frac{1}{2}$	$\frac{3}{4}$	1
0%	25%	50%	75%	100%

★ ANALYZING A ★
NEWSPAPER

Choose a local newspaper.
List categories for items
in the paper. What percent
of the paper is used for
each category?

Category	Percent of the Newspaper
News Stories	
Ads	
Photos + Art	

TWIN VALLEY SCHOOL

Use the percent chart you made. How can you design an 8-page newspaper layout with the same percents?

CheckYOURSELF

Great job! The layout you designed had approximately the same percents for each category. You explained clearly in writing how percents were used in creating your layout.

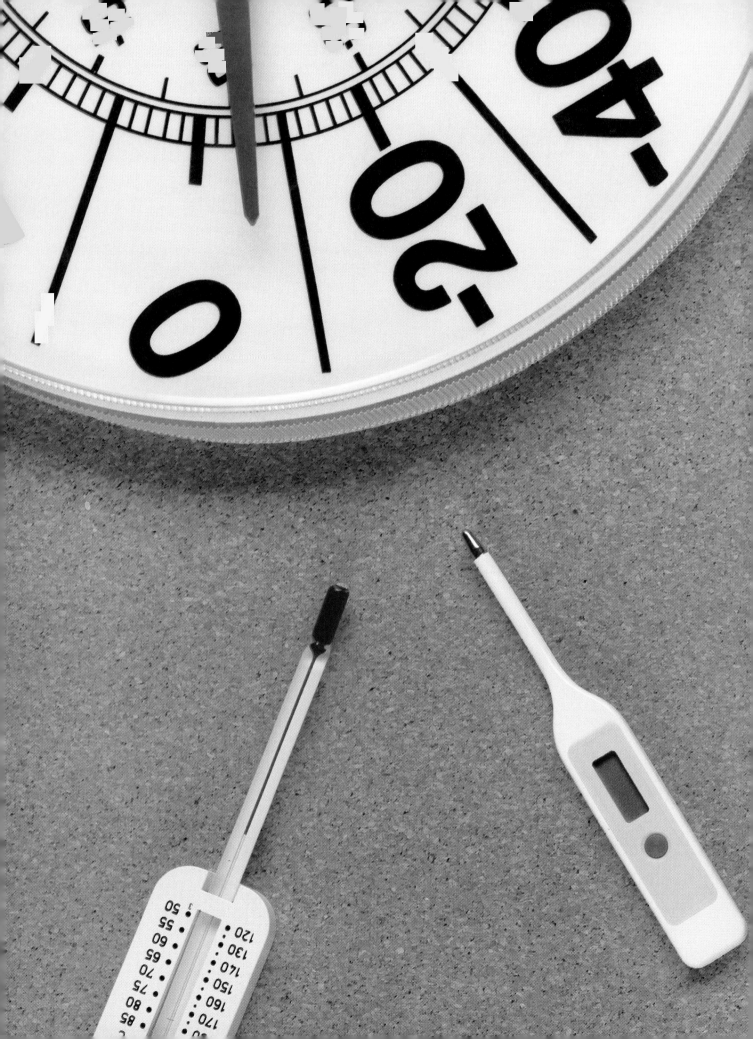

How can we
use negative
numbers?

147

It's a Matter of Degree

TEMPERATURE RANGES OF U.S. CITIES

City	Jan. 10	Jan. 11	Jan. 12
Albany	16/12	19/-3	31/6
Anchorage	4/-12	5/-10	8/-8
Atlanta	46/21	43/24	49/35
Atlantic City	26/15	32/18	40/23
Baton Rouge	53/27	60/36	60/48
Boston	27/17	27/12	36/16
Buffalo	19/7	27/3	37/26
Chattanooga	39/19	46/19	47/30
Chicago	23/-8	33/14	32/27
Cincinnati	28/8	39/15	41/30
Cleveland	21/0	30/5	36/25
Columbus	24/3	34/8	39/27
Denver	40/23	45/19	47/18
Des Moines	19/1	30/18	28/17
Detroit	23/-6	29/5	33/25
El Paso	59/26	58/32	55/27
Honolulu	81/64	81/64	81/64

City	Jan. 10	Jan. 11	Jan. 12
Houston	63/34	68/52	63/56
Indianapolis	27/6	35/13	37/27
Kansas City	39/14	35/31	35/24
Las Vegas	57/30	56/32	57/33
Little Rock	46/21	48/35	49/40
Los Angeles	67/46	73/46	74/46
Memphis	46/24	50/31	52/37
Miami	62/57	70/59	70/66
Milwaukee	24/1	33/15	29/23
Nashville	37/16	48/24	49/34
New Orleans	54/30	61/39	61/50
New York City	25/13	30/13	38/24
Oklahoma City	54/25	52/42	45/30
Omaha	30/5	34/21	33/19
Orlando	66/41	67/46	75/55
Philadelphia	28/17	33/15	40/22
Phoenix	65/39	68/41	68/42

City	Jan. 10	Jan. 11	Jan. 12
Pittsburgh	22/5	31/9	36/25
Providence	24/12	29/8	37/14
Raleigh	37/19	39/18	45/26
Sacramento	56/44	55/37	56/35
St. Louis	37/19	40/26	37/30
Salt Lake City	37/30	38/25	37/21
San Diego	63/45	68/46	69/45
San Francisco	54/48	57/45	57/44
Seattle	49/46	51/42	49/41
Sioux Falls	16/-11	29/12	22/10
Syracuse	15/10	23/-3	35/21
Tampa	65/39	66/41	74/54
Toledo	20/0	30/6	33/26
Tucson	70/39	68/35	67/35
Virginia Beach	35/25	38/22	44/26
Washington D.C.	29/18	34/17	39/24
Wichita	45/24	40/33	43/27

ON YOUR OWN

1. Find and record in a chart the high and low temperatures for your area for the next three days. Get your data from newspapers, the radio or television, or use an outdoor thermometer.

2. In the same chart find and record the temperature difference for each of the days.

3. Write a question you can answer using the data in your chart. Answer the question.

4. *My Journal:* What was most difficult for you in finding differences? Did it have anything to do with whether the numbers were positive or negative? Explain.

Absolutely the
COLDEST

PEOPLE,
SOCIETY, AND
MATHEMATICS

Did you ever wonder how scientists around the world represent temperatures?

Scientists around the world have agreed on many ways to represent data. They use the System International, or SI, for all scientific measurement.

In SI, temperature is represented on the Kelvin scale named after the British scientist, Lord Kelvin.

Here's how the scales compare:

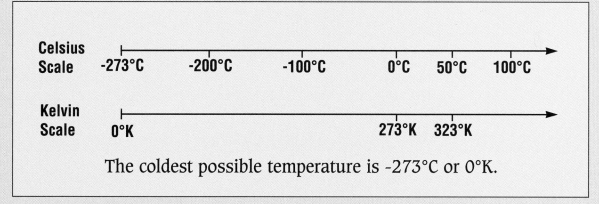

The coldest possible temperature is -273°C or 0°K.

....

1 Are there any negative integers on the Kelvin scale? Explain.

2 How do the sizes of the units on each scale relate?

3 Why do you think scientists decided to use the Kelvin scale?

4 Which temperature scales do you use?

149

Playing an INTEGER Game

Work with your partner to make your own integer game. Other students will play the game you design.

- Put any of the numbers -3, -2, -1, +1, +2, +3 in each of the large circles on the game board.

- Make a spinner to use for your game. You can use one like the one shown or you can make your own spinner.

- Decide on the goal of the game. You might agree that the player closest to the last circle after 5 turns is the winner.

- Decide what happens if there is a tie. Should the players keep playing until one wins? Should they start a new game? Is there some other possibility?

Make sure the rules you write are clear.

- Decide on a name for your game.

Check YOURSELF

Great job! Your integer game is interesting for other students to play. The playing rules are clearly written You wrote to explain how integers are used in your game.

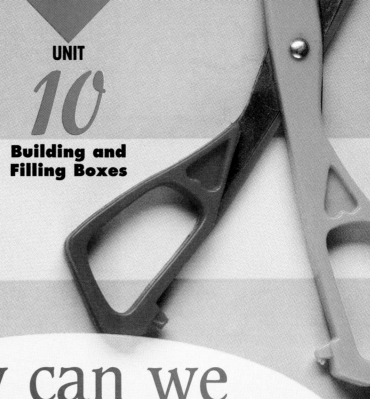

*H*ow can we describe and build boxes?

Boxes, Boxes, Boxes!

What is different about these boxes? What is the same?
What do you think might be in each of the boxes?

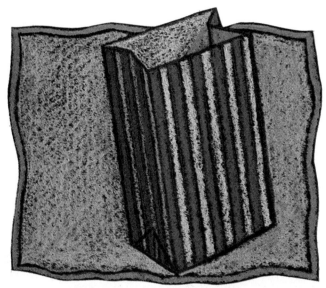

AMAZING
F A C T S

*If you have a cone and a cylinder with the same height
and base, the volume of the cone is only $\frac{1}{3}$ of that of
the cylinder.*

Bigger (and Better?) Boxes

What size open-top box can you build to hold the greatest number of centimeter cubes? How many do you think will fit in each box? Estimate. Tell how you made your estimate.

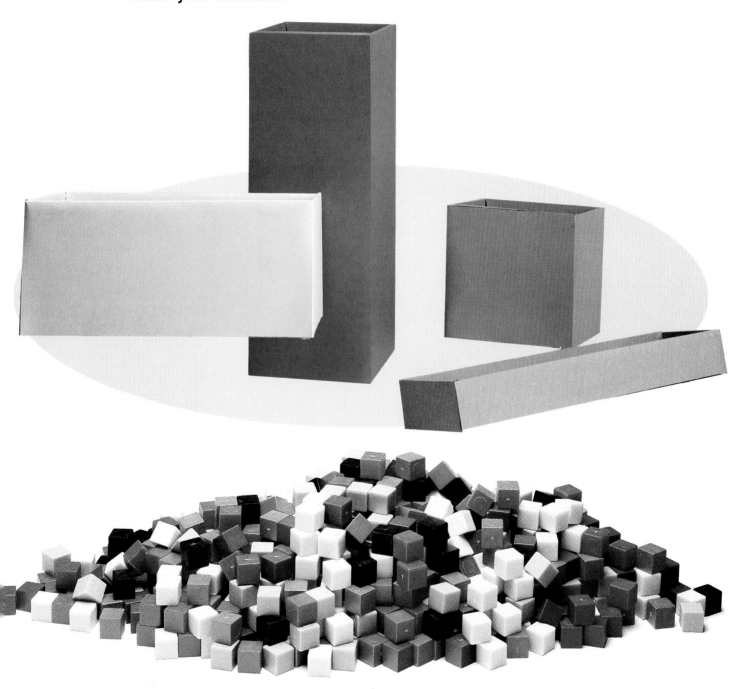

After you have built your own box, show the class data on a line plot.

ON
YOUR
OWN

1. Look at these boxes. How many other boxes can you draw with a volume of 100 cubic centimeters? Label the dimensions of each. Make all dimensions whole numbers.

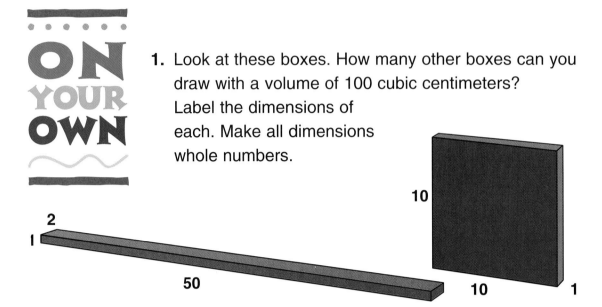

2

1

50

10

10

1

2. The volume of a box is 80 cubic centimeters. One dimension is 5 centimeters. What are some possible numbers for the missing dimensions?

How many blocks are there all together in each block "building?" Write and tell how you decided.

3.

4.

5.

6. *My Journal:* Is the tallest box always the box with the greatest volume? Explain how you know.

Volumes: Change or No Change

▶ Are there other ways to arrange the cubes shown?
Tell how you decided.

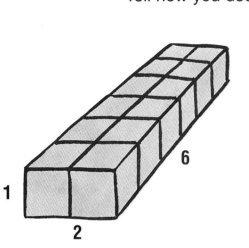

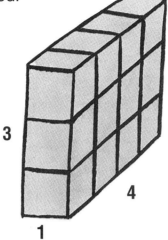

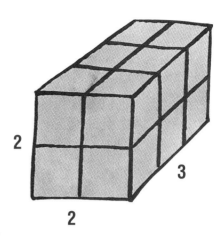

▶ In each pair, are the boxes the same or different?
Write and tell how you decided.

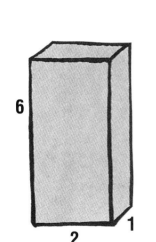

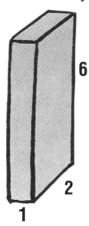

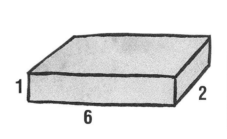

AMAZING
F A C T S

*One of the smallest computers in existence
measures only 7.2 x 2.8 x 0.6 inches. It
would fit inside a regular business envelope.*

ON YOUR OWN

1. Suppose you want to build a box with 100 cubes and you want to put 20 cubes in the bottom layer. How many layers of cubes will you need? Is there more than one set of possible dimensions for this box? What are the possible dimensions?

2. Will a box that is made with 4 layers of 16 cubes have a greater volume than a box made with 8 layers of 8 cubes? Explain your answer.

3. What do you think will happen to the volume if:

    a. the length of a box is doubled and the width and height are not changed?

    b. the width is doubled, and the length and height are not changed?

    c. the height is doubled, and the width and length are not changed?

    What happens to the volume when all three dimensions are doubled?

4. What do you think will happen to the volume if:

    a. the length of a box is tripled, and the width and height are not changed?

    b. the width is tripled, and the length and height are not changed?

    c. the height is tripled, and the width and length are not changed?

    What happens to the volume when all three dimensions are tripled?

5. *My Journal:* Tell how the number of cubes in the bottom layer is related to the total number of cubes in a box. Draw diagrams to show your explanation.

ll Folded Up

▶ Can each pattern be folded to make an open-top box?

► Can the pattern be folded to make a closed-top box? If not, why not?

1.

2.

3.

4.

5. Draw a hexomino that can be folded to make a box. Don't use one from above.

6. *My Journal:* What have you learned about square patterns and boxes?

Wrap It Up

1

2

3

23 in.

18 in.

12 in.

6.5 in.

4.5 in.

PACK THEM IN

H ave you ever wondered about how people decide on packaging materials for shipping?

Have you ever eaten any of these fruits? How did they taste?

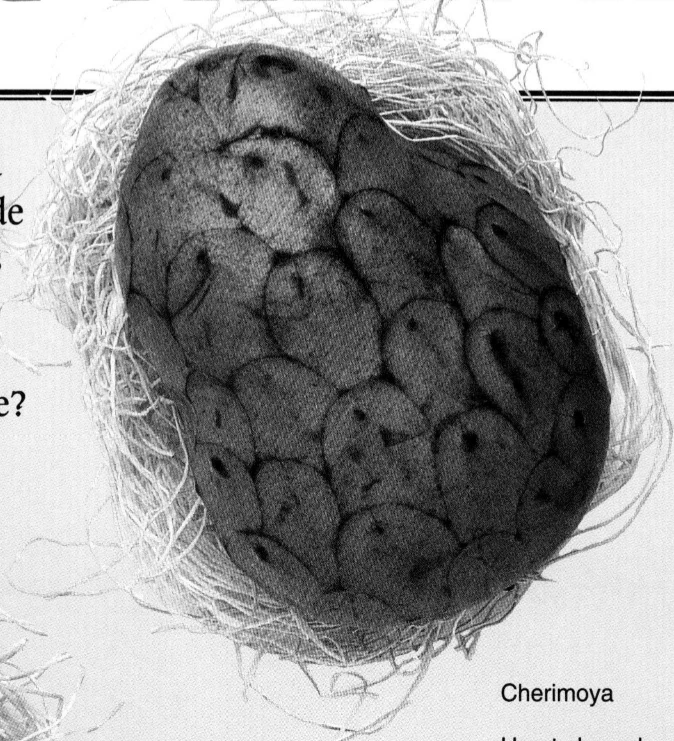

Cherimoya

Heart-shaped

Very tasty when ripe.

Native to the Andes Mountains. Grown in Chile and along the California coast.

Size: about the same as a person's fist.

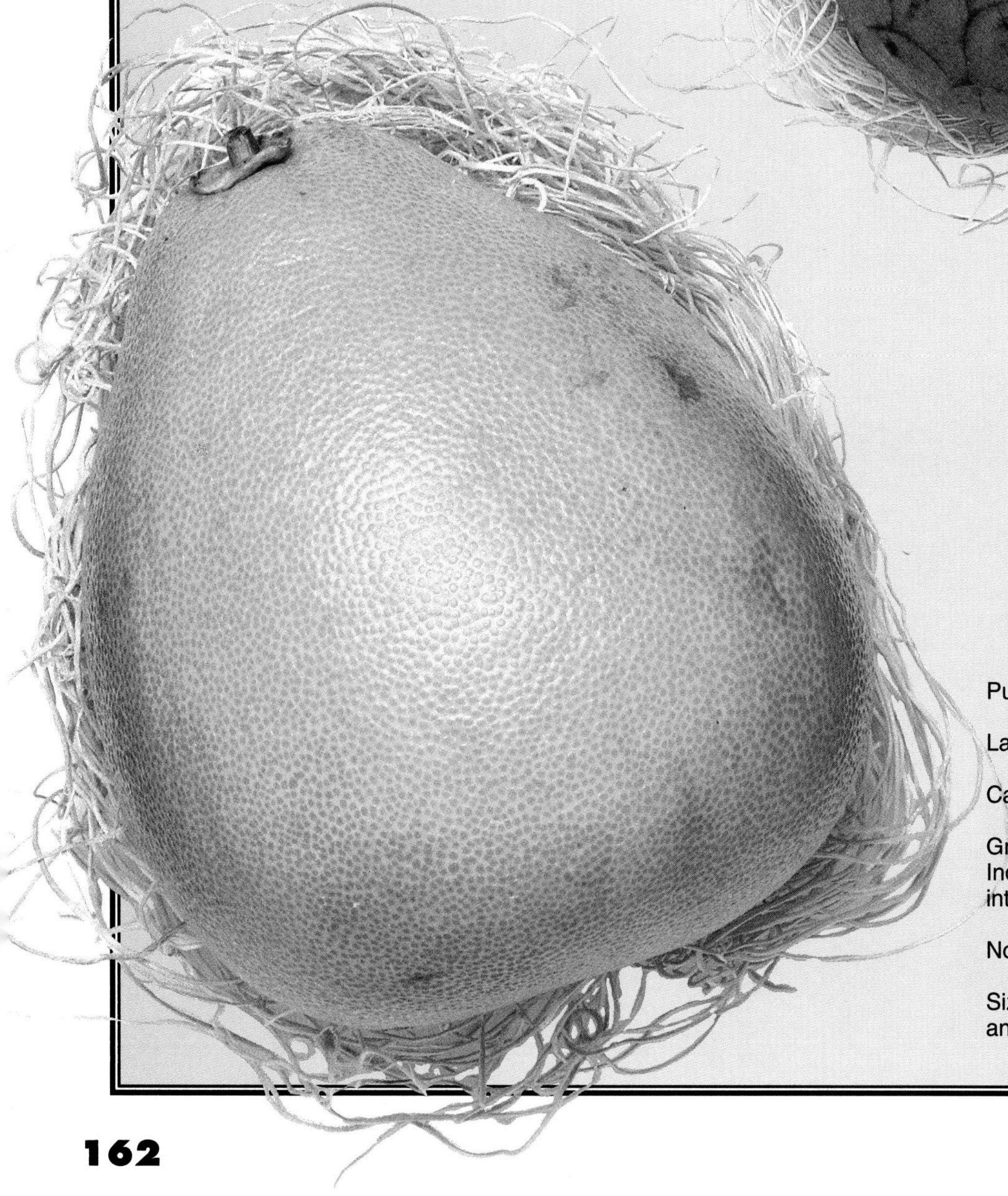

Pummelos

Largest citrus fruit.

Can be round or pear-shaped.

Grown in Southeast Asia: India, China, Indonesia, and introduced to the West Indies.

Now also grown in Israel.

Size: between a grapefruit and a basketball.

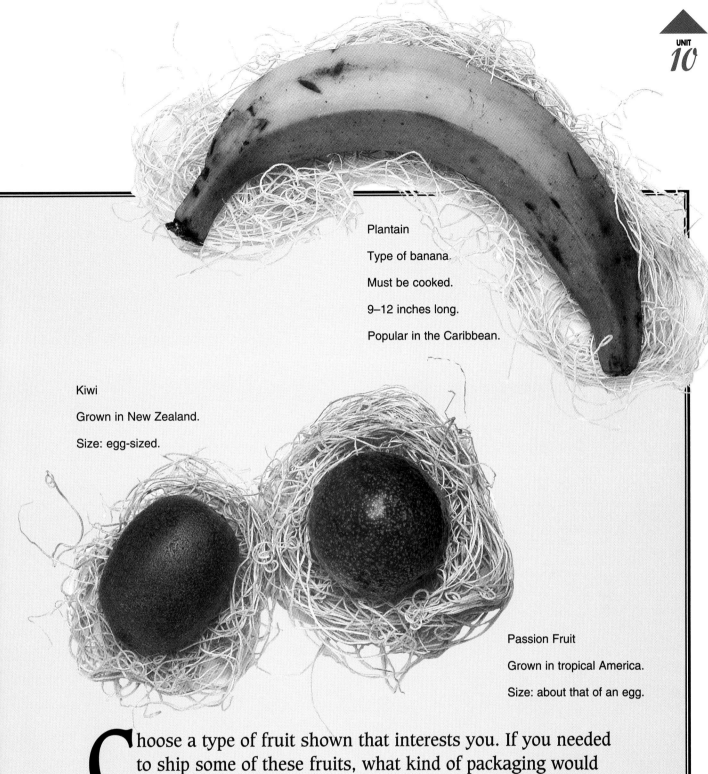

Plantain

Type of banana.

Must be cooked.

9–12 inches long.

Popular in the Caribbean.

Kiwi

Grown in New Zealand.

Size: egg-sized.

Passion Fruit

Grown in tropical America.

Size: about that of an egg.

Choose a type of fruit shown that interests you. If you needed to ship some of these fruits, what kind of packaging would you consider? First decide how many you are shipping. Do you think they will bruise easily? Should there be dividers between them? What kind of packaging for fruit have you seen? Design your package, giving its dimensions. If you were sending your fruit to another country, how might you ship it? Is it important to consider the time involved in shipping?

BUILDING A BOX

What size box will hold 1,000 pencils?

How many boxes are needed to hold 100?

Think about how you planned the box for 1,000 pencils. How would your approach to this problem change if the box were for

- 1,000 erasers?

- 1,000 paper clips?

- 1,000 oranges?

- 1,000 pairs of shoes?

- 1,000 baseball caps?

How would you adjust your box if some items were breakable?

Check YOURSELF

Great job! The box you designed and built held 1,000 pencils without too much wasted space. The net for the box was neat and accurate. You were able to communicate your plans for the box clearly in writing.

*W*hen are shapes similar?

Right Triangles

Congo

Antiqua & Barbuda

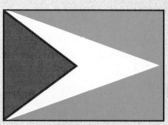
Guyana

Lesotho

Marshall Islands

St. Lucia

Sudan

Trinidad & Tobago

United Kingdom

MAKING A
SIMILAR RIGHT
TRIANGLE

ON YOUR OWN

F   O   Y   M   V   Z

1. Ships sometimes use alphabet flags to communicate. Find all the right triangles in these nautical flags.

2. Look at each pair of triangles. Write to tell if they are similar, congruent, or neither, and why you think so.

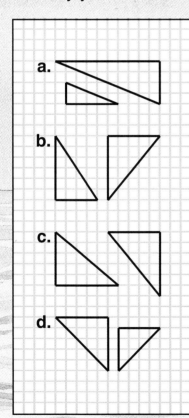

a.

b.

c.

d.

3. Use grid paper to draw any irregular-shaped polygon. Then make a similar figure that is larger or smaller than the original.

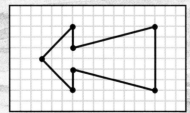

4. *My Journal:* What have you learned about similar and congruent triangles?

What's Your Angle?

1. How many triangles can you find in this pattern? How many are similar? How many are congruent?

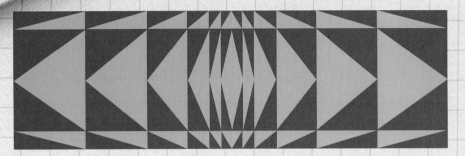

2. Look at each pair of triangles. Write to tell if they are similar, congruent, or neither, and how you know.

a.

b.

c.

d.

3. Trace triangle a. Draw the triangle described in b. Write to tell if the triangles are similar and how you determined your answer.

a.

b. This triangle has one angle of 35° and one angle of 45°. One side measures 4 inches.

4. *My Journal:* Is there anything you don't understand about similar triangles? Explain.

Same Shape,

Did you ever wonder whether people use similar figures and patterns in the arts?

The most popular rectangle with artists and architects throughout history is the "golden rectangle." The width of a golden rectangle is approximately $\frac{3}{5}$ of its length. Any rectangle with this ratio is a golden rectangle, and all golden rectangles are similar. The base of the Great Pyramid of Gizeh built in Egypt 4,600 years ago is a golden rectangle, as are the base of the Parthenon in Greece, and the United Nations Building in New York City. The billions of 3 x 5 cards used in classrooms and offices all over the world are also golden rectangles.

Other examples of similar figures in art are the Russian stacking dolls called metroshkas. Metroshkas are a set of five or more painted wooden dolls, each one small enough to fit inside the next one. The dolls have similar designs and features.

Different Size

1 Find and draw some rectangular objects that have the golden ratios. Explain why they are all similar.

2 Find some similar objects like the dolls. Draw them and explain why they are similar.

3 Make a design for a set of similar objects. Be as creative as you can.

173

Similar Flags?

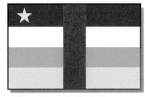

Central African Republic **Costa Rica** **Finland**

1. Find all the rectangles in these flags. Which rectangles are similar? Which are congruent? How did you decide?

2. Look at each pair of rectangles. Write to tell if they are similar, congruent, or neither, and how you decided.

a.

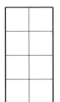

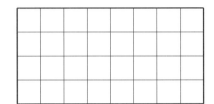

b.

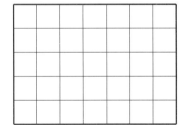

3. Use grid paper to make an interesting design using any number of similar rectangles. You may want to color your design to make it more interesting.

4. *My Journal:* What did you learn that was new?

Going around in Quadrilaterals

1. How many squares can you find in the pattern? Tell which are similar and which are congruent. How many rectangles can you find? Tell which are similar and which are congruent.

2. Look at each pair of quadrilaterals. Write to tell if they are similar, congruent, or neither, and how you know.

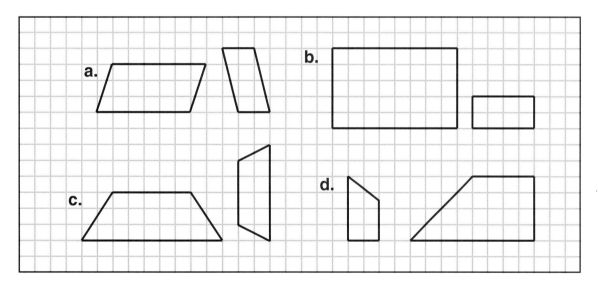

3. Draw a 5- or 6-sided polygon. Then construct a polygon that is similar to it but larger or smaller. Write to tell how you know your figures are similar.

4. *My Journal:* What have you learned about similar quadrilaterals? Do you have any questions? Explain.

MAKING A CLASS MURAL

Similar or not similar?
Compare the two murals.
How many differences
can you find?

How can we make a
class mural?

Work with your group to make
a small design for one part of
the mural. Then you will need
to find a way to enlarge the
small design and incorporate
your work in the class mural.

Check **YOURSELF**

Great job! Your part of the mural was interesting
and used a variety of geometric shapes. You explained
clearly in writing why the shapes in the small design
were similar to those in the enlargement. And, you wrote
clearly to tell how you used similarity to enlarge figures.

Acknowledgments

ILLUSTRATION

Cover Illustration: **Seymour Chwast**
Shelly Bartek: 22, 23; **Karen Bell:** 154; **Jennifer Bolten:** 85-87; **Elizabeth Brady:** 5, 6; **Nan Brooks:** 18, 19;
Roger Chandler: 13-15, 34, 35; **Bradley Clark:** 168, 169; **Darius Detwiler:** 88, 89; **John Edens:** 47;
Pam-ela Harrelson: 62, 63, 140-142; **Jennifer Hewitson:** 42, 66; **Victoria Kahn:** 50; **Lisa Leleu:** 71;
Albert Lemant: 64, 65; **Cheryl Kirk Noll:** 2, 3; **Evan Polenghi:** 29, 30, 32, 33, 124, 125, 157, 158;
Mike Reagan: 100-102; **Mike Reed:** 103-105, 118; **Meryl Rosner:** 32, 33; **Jane Sanders:** 48, 49;
R.M. Schneider: 130, 131; **Remy Simard:** 80, 81; **Scott Snow:** 97-99; **Russ Steffens:** 168, 169, 175;
Steve Sullivan: 176, 177; **Vicki Wehrman:** 82, 83, 159; **Terry Widener:** 55.

PHOTOGRAPHY

Photo Management and Picture Research: **Omni-Photo Communications, Inc.**
Claire Aich: 128, 129, 132, 133, 144, 145; ©Fran Allan/Animals, Animals: 106; ©Philip Jon Bailey/Stock
Boston: 84; ©M. Bertinettti/Photo Researchers: 72; ©Berenholtz/The Stock Market: 31;
©Carmerique/H. Armstrong Roberts: 32; ©Commet/Leo DeWys: 141; ©Greig Cranna/Stock Boston: 84;
©Culver Pictures, Inc.: 12, 149; ©Bob Daemmrich/Stock Boston: 72; ©Jay Dorin/Omni-Photo
Communications: 126; ©Explorer/Photo Researchers: 72; **Everett Studios:** 26, 27, 36, 38, 56, 58, 72-75, 90,
91, 114, 115, 126, 127, 166, 167, 178, 179; ©Barry Fanton: 148; ©Focus on Sports: 75; ©The Granger
Collection: 109; ©Gilbert Garcia/The Image Bank: 172; ©Mickey Gibson/Animals, Animals: 106, 107; **Michael
Groen:** 1, 24, 32, 33, 66-68, 92, 93, 103, 105, 112, 113, 122, 123, 146, 147, 150-153, 161, 164, 165, 174;
Horizon: 2-4, 7-10, 18, 20, 21, 119-121; **Richard Hutchings:** 28, 94, 108, 110, 116, 117; **Ken Karp:** 40, 41, 51,
70, 95, 96, 154-156, 159, 162, 163, 170, 172, 173, 176; ©Ken Karp/Omni-Photo Communications: 157;
©Marcia Keegan/The Stock Market: 31; ©Stephen J. Kransemann/Photo Researchers: 53;
©R. Krubner/H. Armstrong Roberts: 136; ©Leonard Lee Rue III/Photo Researchers: 106; **John Lei:** 17, 46, 47,
54, 140, 168, 169; ©Ted Levin/Earth Scenes: 44; ©Rafael Macia/Photo Researchers: 134,135;
©Tom McHugh/Animals, Animals: 107; ©Meyers/Okapia/Photo Researchers: 107; ©The Newark Museum: 16;
©Nick Nicholson/The Image Bank: 31; ©Hans Pfletschinger/Peter Arnold Inc.: 52; ©Steve Niedorf/The Image
Bank: 109; ©Pictor/Uniphoto: 30; ©Ranjitsinh/Photo Researchers: 107; ©Co Rentmeester/The Image Bank: 2;
©Dennis Stock/Magnum Photos: 31; **Superstock:** 43; ©Paul Trummer/The Image Bank: 3; ©Tom Van
Sant/The Stock Market: 130; ©Fred Whitehead/Animals, Animals: 106; ©Jack Wilburn/Earth Scenes: 72.

CALCULATORS

T-I 108
T-I Math Explorer

MANIPULATIVES

Link-its ™
Power Polygons